Book of
PSALMS

ROSE
PUBLISHING

Book of Psalms

© 2014 Bristol Works, Inc.

Published by Rose Publishing
An imprint of Hendrickson Publishing Group
Rose Publishing, LLC
P.O. Box 3473
Peabody, Massachusetts 01961-3473
www.HendricksonPublishingGroup.com

ISBN 978-1-62862-083-2

New American Standard Bible. Copyright © 1960, 1962, 1963, 1968, 1971, 1972, 1973, 1975, 1977, 1995 by The Lockman Foundation. La Habra, Calif. All rights reserved. www.Lockman.org

Printed in the United States of America

February 2021, 5th printing

THE PSALMS

The following expressions occur often in the Psalms:

Selah	May mean *Pause, Crescendo* or *Musical Interlude*
Maskil	Possibly, *Contemplative,* or *Didactic,* or *Skillful Psalm*
Mikhtam	Possibly, *Epigrammatic Poem,* or *Atonement Psalm*
Sheol	The nether world

BOOK 1

PSALM 1

The Righteous and the Wicked Contrasted.

1 How blessed is the man who does not walk in the counsel of the wicked,
Nor stand in the path of sinners,
Nor sit in the seat of scoffers!
2 But his delight is in the law of the LORD,
And in His law he meditates day and night.
3 He will be like a tree *firmly* planted by streams of water,
Which yields its fruit in its season
And its leaf does not wither;
And in whatever he does, he prospers.
4 The wicked are not so,
But they are like chaff which the wind drives away.
5 Therefore the wicked will not stand in the judgment,
Nor sinners in the assembly of the righteous.
6 For the LORD knows the way of the righteous,
But the way of the wicked will perish.

PSALM 2

The Reign of the LORD'S Anointed.

1 Why are the nations in an uproar
And the peoples devising a vain thing?
2 The kings of the earth take their stand
And the rulers take counsel together
Against the LORD and against His [1]Anointed, saying,
3 "Let us tear their fetters apart
And cast away their cords from us!"
4 He who [2]sits in the heavens laughs,
The Lord scoffs at them.
5 Then He will speak to them in His anger
And terrify them in His fury, saying,
6 "But as for Me, I have installed My King
Upon Zion, My holy mountain."
7 "I will surely tell of the decree of the LORD:
He said to Me, 'You are My Son,
Today I have begotten You.
8 'Ask of Me, and I will surely

1. Or *Messiah* 2. Or *is enthroned*

3

give the nations as Your
inheritance,
And the *very* ends of the earth
as Your possession.

9 'You shall [1]break them with a
rod of iron,
You shall shatter them like
earthenware.' "

10 Now therefore, O kings, show
discernment;
Take warning, O [2]judges of
the earth.

11 Worship the LORD with
reverence
And rejoice with trembling.

12 Do homage to the Son, that
He not become angry, and
you perish *in* the way,
For His wrath may [3]soon be
kindled.
How blessed are all who take
refuge in Him!

PSALM 3

Morning Prayer of Trust in God.
A Psalm of David, when he fled
from Absalom his son.

1 O LORD, how my adversaries
have increased!
Many are rising up against
me.

2 Many are saying of my soul,
"There is no deliverance for
him in God."   [4]Selah.

3 But You, O LORD, are a shield
about me,
My glory, and the One who
lifts my head.

4 I was crying to the LORD with
my voice,
And He answered me from
His holy mountain.   Selah.

5 I lay down and slept;
I awoke, for the LORD sustains
me.

6 I will not be afraid of ten
thousands of people
Who have set themselves
against me round about.

7 Arise, O LORD; save me, O my
God!
For You have smitten all my
enemies on the cheek;
You have shattered the teeth
of the wicked.

8 Salvation belongs to the LORD;
Your blessing *be* upon Your
people!   Selah.

PSALM 4

Evening Prayer of Trust in God.
For the choir director; on stringed
instruments. A Psalm of David.

1 Answer me when I call, O God
of my righteousness!
You have relieved me in my
distress;
Be gracious to me and hear
my prayer.

2 O sons of men, how long will
my honor become a
reproach?
How long will you love what is
worthless and aim at
deception?   Selah.

3 But know that the LORD has
set apart the godly man for
Himself;
The LORD hears when I call to
Him.

4 Tremble, and do not sin;
Meditate in your heart upon
your bed, and be still.   Selah.

5 Offer the sacrifices of
righteousness,
And trust in the LORD.

6 Many are saying, "Who will
show us *any* good?"
Lift up the light of Your

---

1. Another reading is *rule* 2. Or *leaders* 3. Or *quickly, suddenly, easily* 4. *Selah* may
mean: *Pause, Crescendo* or *Musical interlude*

countenance upon us, O
LORD!
7 You have put gladness in my
heart,
More than when their grain
and new wine abound.
8 In peace I will both lie down
and sleep,
For You alone, O LORD, make
me to dwell in safety.

PSALM 5

*Prayer for Protection
from the Wicked.*
For the choir director;
for flute accompaniment.
A Psalm of David.

1 Give ear to my words, O LORD,
Consider my ¹groaning.
2 Heed the sound of my cry for
help, my King and my God,
For to You I pray.
3 In the morning, O LORD, You
will hear my voice;
In the morning I will order *my
prayer* to You and *eagerly*
watch.
4 For You are not a God who
takes pleasure in wickedness;
No evil dwells with You.
5 The boastful shall not stand
before Your eyes;
You hate all who do iniquity.
6 You destroy those who speak
falsehood;
The LORD abhors the man of
bloodshed and deceit.
7 But as for me, by Your
abundant lovingkindness I
will enter Your house,
At Your holy temple I will
bow in reverence for You.
8 O LORD, lead me in Your
righteousness because of my
foes;

Make Your way straight
before me.
9 There is nothing reliable in
what they say;
Their inward part is
destruction *itself.*
Their throat is an open grave;
They flatter with their tongue.
10 Hold them guilty, O God;
By their own devices let them
fall!
In the multitude of their
transgressions thrust them
out,
For they are rebellious against
You.
11 But let all who take refuge in
You be glad,
Let them ever sing for joy;
And may You shelter them,
That those who love Your
name may exult in You.
12 For it is You who blesses the
righteous man, O LORD,
You surround him with favor
as with a shield.

PSALM 6

*Prayer for Mercy in
Time of Trouble.*
For the choir director; with
stringed instruments, upon
an eight-string lyre.
A Psalm of David.

1 O LORD, do not rebuke me in
Your anger,
Nor chasten me in Your
wrath.
2 Be gracious to me, O LORD, for
I *am* pining away;
Heal me, O LORD, for my
bones are dismayed.
3 And my soul is greatly
dismayed;
But You, O LORD—how long?

---

1. Or *meditation*

5

4 Return, O Lᴏʀᴅ, rescue my
¹soul;
Save me because of Your
lovingkindness.
5 For there is no ²mention of
You in death;
In Sheol who will give You
thanks?
6 I am weary with my sighing;
Every night I make my bed
swim,
I dissolve my couch with my
tears.
7 My eye has wasted away with
grief;
It has become old because of
all my adversaries.
8 Depart from me, all you who
do iniquity,
For the Lᴏʀᴅ has heard the
voice of my weeping.
9 The Lᴏʀᴅ has heard my
supplication,
The Lᴏʀᴅ receives my prayer.
10 All my enemies will be
ashamed and greatly
dismayed;
They shall turn back, they will
suddenly be ashamed.

PSALM 7

*The Lᴏʀᴅ Implored to Defend the
Psalmist against the Wicked.*
A ³Shiggaion of David, which he
sang to the Lᴏʀᴅ concerning
Cush, a Benjamite.

1 O Lᴏʀᴅ my God, in You I
have taken refuge;
Save me from all those who
pursue me, and deliver me,
2 Or he will tear my soul like a
lion,
Dragging me away, while
there is none to deliver.

3 O Lᴏʀᴅ my God, if I have
done this,
If there is injustice in my
hands,
4 If I have rewarded evil to my
friend,
Or have plundered him who
without cause was my
adversary,
5 Let the enemy pursue my soul
and overtake *it;*
And let him trample my life
down to the ground
And lay my glory in the dust.
Selah.
6 Arise, O Lᴏʀᴅ, in Your anger;
Lift up Yourself against the
rage of my adversaries,
And arouse Yourself for me;
You have appointed
judgment.
7 Let the assembly of the
peoples encompass You,
And over them return on high.
8 The Lᴏʀᴅ judges the peoples;
Vindicate me, O Lᴏʀᴅ,
according to my
righteousness and my
integrity that is in me.
9 O let the evil of the wicked
come to an end, but establish
the righteous;
For the righteous God tries the
hearts and ⁴minds.
10 My shield is with God,
Who saves the upright in
heart.
11 God is a righteous judge,
And a God who has
indignation every day.
12 If a man does not repent, He
will sharpen His sword;
He has bent His bow and
made it ready.

1. Or *life* 2. Or *remembrance* 3. I.e. Dithyrambic rhythm; or wild passionate song
4. Lit *kidneys,* figurative for inner man

6

13 He has also prepared for
   Himself deadly weapons;
   He makes His arrows fiery
   shafts.
14 Behold, he travails with
   wickedness,
   And he conceives mischief and
   brings forth falsehood.
15 He has dug a pit and hollowed
   it out,
   And has fallen into the hole
   which he made.
16 His mischief will return upon
   his own head,
   And his violence will descend
   upon ¹his own pate.
17 I will give thanks to the LORD
   according to His
   righteousness
   And will sing praise to the
   name of the LORD Most High.

PSALM 8

*The LORD's Glory and
Man's Dignity.*
For the choir director; on the
Gittith. A Psalm of David.

1 O LORD, our Lord,
   How majestic is Your name in
   all the earth,
   Who have displayed Your
   splendor above the heavens!
2 From the mouth of infants
   and nursing babes You have
   established strength
   Because of Your adversaries,
   To make the enemy and the
   revengeful cease.
3 When I consider Your
   heavens, the work of Your
   fingers,
   The moon and the stars,
   which You have ordained;
4 What is man that You take
   thought of him,

   And the son of man that You
   care for him?
5 Yet You have made him a
   little lower than God,
   And You crown him with
   glory and majesty!
6 You make him to rule over the
   works of Your hands;
   You have put all things under
   his feet,
7 All sheep and oxen,
   And also the beasts of the
   field,
8 The birds of the heavens and
   the fish of the sea,
   Whatever passes through the
   paths of the seas.
9 O LORD, our Lord,
   How majestic is Your name in
   all the earth!

PSALM 9

*A Psalm of Thanksgiving
for God's Justice.*
For the choir director; on
²Muth-labben. A Psalm of David.

1 I will give thanks to the LORD
   with all my heart;
   I will tell of all Your wonders.
2 I will be glad and exult in You;
   I will sing praise to Your
   name, O Most High.
3 When my enemies turn back,
   They stumble and perish
   before You.
4 For You have maintained my
   just cause;
   You have sat on the throne
   judging righteously.
5 You have rebuked the nations,
   You have destroyed the
   wicked;
   You have blotted out their
   name forever and ever.

---

1. I.e. the crown of his own head   2. I.e. "Death to the Son"

6 The enemy has come to an
end in perpetual ruins,
And You have uprooted the
cities;
The very memory of them has
perished.

7 But the LORD [1]abides forever;
He has established His throne
for judgment,

8 And He will judge the world
in righteousness;
He will execute judgment for
the peoples with equity.

9 The LORD also will be a
stronghold for the oppressed,
A stronghold in times of
trouble;

10 And those who know Your
name will put their trust in
You,
For You, O LORD, have not
forsaken those who seek You.

11 Sing praises to the LORD, who
dwells in Zion;
Declare among the peoples
His deeds.

12 For He who [2]requires blood
remembers them;
He does not forget the cry of
the afflicted.

13 Be gracious to me, O LORD;
See my affliction from those
who hate me,
You who lift me up from the
gates of death,

14 That I may tell of all Your
praises,
That in the gates of the
daughter of Zion
I may rejoice in Your
salvation.

15 The nations have sunk down
in the pit which they have
made;
In the net which they hid,

their own foot has been
caught.

16 The LORD has made Himself
known;
He has executed judgment.
In the work of his own hands
the wicked is snared.
                    Higgaion Selah.

17 The wicked will return to
Sheol,
Even all the nations who
forget God.

18 For the needy will not always
be forgotten,
Nor the hope of the afflicted
perish forever.

19 Arise, O LORD, do not let man
prevail;
Let the nations be judged
before You.

20 Put them in fear, O LORD;
Let the nations know that they
are but men.   Selah.

PSALM 10

*A Prayer for the Overthrow
of the Wicked.*

1 Why do You stand afar off, O
LORD?
Why do You hide *Yourself* in
times of trouble?

2 In pride the wicked hotly
pursue the afflicted;
Let them be caught in the
plots which they have
devised.

3 For the wicked boasts of his
heart's desire,
And [3]the greedy man curses
and spurns the LORD.

4 The wicked, in the
haughtiness of his
countenance, does not seek
Him.

1. Or *sits* as king   2. I.e. avenges bloodshed   3. Or *blesses the greedy man*

8

All his thoughts are, "There is no God."

5 His ways prosper at all times;
Your judgments are on high, out of his sight;
As for all his adversaries, he snorts at them.

6 He says to himself, "I will not be moved;
Throughout all generations I will not be in adversity."

7 His mouth is full of curses and deceit and oppression;
Under his tongue is mischief and wickedness.

8 He sits in the lurking places of the villages;
In the hiding places he kills the innocent;
His eyes stealthily watch for the unfortunate.

9 He lurks in a hiding place as a lion in his lair;
He lurks to catch the afflicted;
He catches the afflicted when he draws him into his net.

10 He crouches, he bows down,
And the unfortunate fall ¹by his mighty ones.

11 He says to himself, "God has forgotten;
He has hidden His face; He will never see it."

12 Arise, O LORD; O God, lift up Your hand.
Do not forget the afflicted.

13 Why has the wicked spurned God?
He has said to himself, "You will not require it."

14 You have seen it, for You have beheld mischief and vexation
to take it into Your hand.
The unfortunate commits himself to You;

You have been the helper of the orphan.

15 Break the arm of the wicked and the evildoer,
Seek out his wickedness until You find none.

16 The LORD is King forever and ever;
Nations have perished from His land.

17 O LORD, You have heard the desire of the ²humble;
You will strengthen their heart, You will incline Your ear

18 To ³vindicate the orphan and the oppressed,
So that man who is of the earth will no longer cause terror.

PSALM 11

The LORD a Refuge and Defense.
For the choir director.
A Psalm of David.

1 In the LORD I take refuge;
How can you say to my soul,
"Flee *as* a bird to your mountain;

2 For, behold, the wicked bend the bow,
They make ready their arrow upon the string
To shoot in darkness at the upright in heart.

3 If the foundations are destroyed,
What can the righteous do?"

4 The LORD is in His holy temple; the LORD's throne is in heaven;
His eyes behold, His eyelids test the sons of men.

5 The LORD tests the righteous and the wicked,

1. Or *into his claws* 2. Or *afflicted* 3. Lit *judge*

And the one who loves
violence His soul hates.
6 Upon the wicked He will rain
^{1}snares;
Fire and brimstone and
burning wind will be the
portion of their cup.
7 For the Lord is righteous, He
loves righteousness;
The upright will behold His
face.

PSALM 12

*God, a Helper against
the Treacherous.*
For the choir director; upon
an eight-stringed lyre.
A Psalm of David.

1 Help, Lord, for the godly man
ceases to be,
For the faithful disappear
from among the sons of men.
2 They speak falsehood to one
another;
With flattering lips and with a
double heart they speak.
3 May the Lord cut off all
flattering lips,
The tongue that speaks great
things;
4 Who have said, "With our
tongue we will prevail;
Our lips are our own; who is
lord over us?"
5 "Because of the devastation of
the afflicted, because of the
groaning of the needy,
Now I will arise," says the
Lord; "I will set him in the
safety for which he longs."
6 The words of the Lord are
pure words;
As silver tried in a furnace on
the earth, refined seven times.
7 You, O Lord, will keep them;

You will preserve him from
this generation forever.
8 The wicked strut about on
every side
When ^{2}vileness is exalted
among the sons of men.

PSALM 13

Prayer for Help in Trouble.
For the choir director.
A Psalm of David.

1 How long, O Lord? Will You
forget me forever?
How long will You hide Your
face from me?
2 How long shall I take counsel
in my soul,
Having sorrow in my heart all
the day?
How long will my enemy be
exalted over me?
3 Consider *and* answer me, O
Lord my God;
Enlighten my eyes, or I will
sleep the *sleep of* death,
4 And my enemy will say, "I
have overcome him,"
And my adversaries will
rejoice when I am shaken.
5 But I have trusted in Your
lovingkindness;
My heart shall rejoice in Your
salvation.
6 I will sing to the Lord,
Because He has dealt
bountifully with me.

PSALM 14

Folly and Wickedness of Men.
For the choir director.
A Psalm of David.

1 The fool has said in his heart,
"There is no God."
They are corrupt, they have
committed abominable deeds;

1. Or *coals of fire* 2. Or *worthlessness*

There is no one who does
good.
2 The Lord has looked down
from heaven upon the sons of
men
To see if there are any who
understand,
Who seek after God.
3 They have all turned aside,
together they have become
corrupt;
There is no one who does
good, not even one.
4 Do all the workers of
wickedness not know,
Who eat up my people *as* they
eat bread,
And do not call upon the
Lord?
5 There they are in great dread,
For God is with the righteous
generation.
6 You would put to shame the
counsel of the afflicted,
But the Lord is his refuge.
7 Oh, that the salvation of Israel
would come out of Zion!
When the Lord [1]restores His
captive people,
Jacob will rejoice, Israel will
be glad.

PSALM 15

Description of a Citizen of Zion.
A Psalm of David.

1 O Lord, who may abide in
Your tent?
Who may dwell on Your holy
hill?
2 He who walks with integrity,
and works righteousness,
And speaks truth in his heart.
3 He does not slander with his
tongue,
Nor does evil to his neighbor,

Nor takes up a reproach
against his friend;
4 In whose eyes a reprobate is
despised,
But who honors those who
fear the Lord;
He swears to his own hurt and
does not change;
5 He does not put out his money
[2]at interest,
Nor does he take a bribe
against the innocent.
He who does these things will
never be shaken.

PSALM 16

*The Lord the Psalmist's Portion
in Life and Deliverer in Death.*
A [3]Mikhtam of David.

1 Preserve me, O God, for I take
refuge in You.
2 I said to the Lord, "You are
my Lord;
I have no good besides You."
3 As for the saints who are in
the earth,
They are the majestic ones in
whom is all my delight.
4 The sorrows of those who have
bartered for another *god* will
be multiplied;
I shall not pour out their drink
offerings of blood,
Nor will I take their names
upon my lips.
5 The Lord is the portion of my
inheritance and my cup;
You support my lot.
6 The lines have fallen to me in
pleasant places;
Indeed, my heritage is
beautiful to me.
7 I will bless the Lord who has
counseled me;

1. Or *restores the fortunes of His people* 2. I.e. to a fellow Israelite 3. Possibly
Epigrammatic Poem or *Atonement Psalm*

Indeed, my mind instructs me in the night.

8 I have set the LORD continually before me;
Because He is at my right hand, I will not be shaken.

9 Therefore my heart is glad and my glory rejoices;
My flesh also will dwell securely.

10 For You will not abandon my soul to Sheol;
Nor will You allow Your Holy One to [1]undergo decay.

11 You will make known to me the path of life;
In Your presence is fullness of joy;
In Your right hand there are pleasures forever.

PSALM 17

Prayer for Protection against Oppressors.
A Prayer of David.

1 Hear a just cause, O LORD, give heed to my cry;
Give ear to my prayer, which is not from deceitful lips.

2 Let my judgment come forth from Your presence;
Let Your eyes look with equity.

3 You have tried my heart;
You have visited *me* by night;
You have tested me and You find [2]nothing;
I have purposed that my mouth will not transgress.

4 As for the deeds of men, by the word of Your lips
I have kept from the paths of the violent.

5 My steps have held fast to Your paths.

My feet have not slipped.

6 I have called upon You, for You will answer me, O God;
Incline Your ear to me, hear my speech.

7 Wondrously show Your lovingkindness,
O Savior of those who take refuge at Your right hand
From those who rise up *against them.*

8 Keep me as [3]the apple of the eye;
Hide me in the shadow of Your wings

9 From the wicked who despoil me,
My deadly enemies who surround me.

10 They have closed their unfeeling *heart,*
With their mouth they speak proudly.

11 They have now surrounded us in our steps;
They set their eyes to cast *us* down to the ground.

12 He is like a lion that is eager to tear,
And as a young lion lurking in hiding places.

13 Arise, O LORD, confront him, bring him low;
Deliver my soul from the wicked with Your sword,

14 From men with Your hand, O LORD,
From men of the world, whose portion is in *this* life,
And whose belly You fill with Your treasure;
They are satisfied with children,
And leave their abundance to their babes.

1. Or *see corruption* or *the pit* 2. Or *no evil device in me; My mouth* 3. Lit *the pupil, the daughter of the eye*

15 As for me, I shall behold Your
   face in righteousness;
   I will be satisfied with Your
   likeness when I awake.

PSALM 18

*The LORD Praised for
Giving Deliverance.*

For the choir director. A *Psalm* of
David the servant of the LORD,
who spoke to the LORD the words
of this song in the day that the
LORD delivered him from the
hand of all his enemies and from
the hand of Saul. And he said,

1 "I love You, O LORD, my
   strength."
2 The LORD is my rock and my
   fortress and my deliverer,
   My God, my rock, in whom I
   take refuge;
   My shield and the horn of my
   salvation, my stronghold.
3 I call upon the LORD, who is
   worthy to be praised,
   And I am saved from my
   enemies.
4 The cords of death
   encompassed me,
   And the torrents of
   ¹ungodliness terrified me.
5 The cords of Sheol surrounded
   me;
   The snares of death
   confronted me.
6 In my distress I called upon
   the LORD,
   And cried to my God for help;
   He heard my voice out of His
   temple,
   And my cry for help before
   Him came into His ears.
7 Then the earth shook and
   quaked;

And the foundations of the
   mountains were trembling
   And were shaken, because He
   was angry.
8 Smoke went up out of His
   nostrils,
   And fire from His mouth
   devoured;
   Coals were kindled by it.
9 He bowed the heavens also,
   and came down
   With thick darkness under
   His feet.
10 He rode upon a cherub and
   flew;
   And He sped upon the wings
   of the wind.
11 He made darkness His hiding
   place, His canopy around
   Him,
   Darkness of waters, thick
   clouds of the skies.
12 From the brightness before
   Him passed His thick clouds,
   Hailstones and coals of fire.
13 The LORD also thundered in
   the heavens,
   And the Most High uttered
   His voice,
   Hailstones and coals of fire.
14 He sent out His arrows, and
   scattered them,
   And lightning flashes in
   abundance, and routed them.
15 Then the channels of water
   appeared,
   And the foundations of the
   world were laid bare
   At Your rebuke, O LORD,
   At the blast of the breath of
   Your nostrils.
16 He sent from on high, He took
   me;
   He drew me out of many
   waters.

---

1. Or *destruction;* Heb *Belial*

17 He delivered me from my
strong enemy,
And from those who hated
me, for they were too mighty
for me.
18 They confronted me in the day
of my calamity,
But the LORD was my stay.
19 He brought me forth also into
a broad place;
He rescued me, because He
delighted in me.
20 The LORD has rewarded me
according to my
righteousness;
According to the cleanness of
my hands He has
recompensed me.
21 For I have kept the ways of
the LORD,
And have not wickedly
departed from my God.
22 For all His ordinances were
before me,
And I did not put away His
statutes from me.
23 I was also ¹blameless with
Him,
And I kept myself from my
iniquity.
24 Therefore the LORD has
recompensed me according to
my righteousness,
According to the cleanness of
my hands in His eyes.
25 With the kind You show
Yourself kind;
With the blameless You show
Yourself blameless;
26 With the pure You show
Yourself pure,
And with the crooked You
show Yourself ²astute.
27 For You save an afflicted
people,
But haughty eyes You abase.

28 For You light my lamp;
The LORD my God illumines
my darkness.
29 For by You I can ³run upon a
troop;
And by my God I can leap
over a wall.
30 As for God, His way is
blameless;
The word of the LORD is tried;
He is a shield to all who take
refuge in Him.
31 For who is God, but the LORD?
And who is a rock, except our
God,
32 The God who girds me with
strength
And makes my way
blameless?
33 He makes my feet like hinds'
feet,
And sets me upon my high
places.
34 He trains my hands for battle,
So that my arms can bend a
bow of bronze.
35 You have also given me the
shield of Your salvation,
And Your right hand upholds
me;
And Your gentleness makes
me great.
36 You enlarge my steps under
me,
And my feet have not slipped.
37 I pursued my enemies and
overtook them,
And I did not turn back until
they were consumed.
38 I shattered them, so that they
were not able to rise;
They fell under my feet.
39 For You have girded me with
strength for battle;
You have subdued under me
those who rose up against me.

1. Lit *complete; or having integrity; or perfect* 2. Lit *twisted* 3. Or *crush a troop*

40 You have also made my
enemies turn their backs to
me,
And I ¹destroyed those who
hated me.
41 They cried for help, but there
was none to save,
Even to the LORD, but He did
not answer them.
42 Then I beat them fine as the
dust before the wind;
I emptied them out as the
mire of the streets.
43 You have delivered me from
the contentions of the people;
You have placed me as head
of the nations;
A people whom I have not
known serve me.
44 As soon as they hear, they
obey me;
Foreigners ²submit to me.
45 Foreigners fade away,
And come trembling out of
their fortresses.
46 The LORD lives, and blessed be
my rock;
And exalted be the God of my
salvation,
47 The God who executes
vengeance for me,
And subdues peoples under
me.
48 He delivers me from my
enemies;
Surely You lift me above those
who rise up against me;
You rescue me from the
violent man.
49 Therefore I will give thanks to
You among the nations, O
LORD,
And I will sing praises to Your
name.

50 He gives great ³deliverance to
His king,
And shows lovingkindness to
His anointed,
To David and his descendants
forever.

PSALM 19

The Works and the Word of God.
For the choir director.
A Psalm of David.

1 The heavens are telling of the
glory of God;
And their expanse is declaring
the work of His hands.
2 Day to day pours forth speech,
And night to night reveals
knowledge.
3 There is no speech, nor are
there words;
Their voice is not heard.
4 Their ⁴line has gone out
through all the earth,
And their utterances to the
end of the world.
In them He has placed a tent
for the sun,
5 Which is as a bridegroom
coming out of his chamber;
It rejoices as a strong man to
run his course.
6 Its rising is from one end of
the heavens,
And its circuit to the other end
of them;
And there is nothing hidden
from its heat.
7 The law of the LORD is
⁵perfect, restoring the soul;
The testimony of the LORD is
sure, making wise the simple.
8 The precepts of the LORD are
right, rejoicing the heart;
The commandment of the

---

1. Or *silenced* 2. Lit *deceive me;* i.e. give feigned obedience 3. I.e. victories; lit
salvations 4. Another reading is *sound* 5. I.e. blameless

LORD is pure, enlightening the
eyes.
9 The fear of the LORD is clean,
enduring forever;
The judgments of the LORD
are true; they are righteous
altogether.
10 They are more desirable than
gold, yes, than much fine
gold;
Sweeter also than honey and
the drippings of the
honeycomb.
11 Moreover, by them Your
servant is warned;
In keeping them there is great
reward.
12 Who can discern *his* errors?
Acquit me of hidden *faults.*
13 Also keep back Your servant
from presumptuous *sins;*
Let them not rule over me;
Then I will be ¹blameless,
And I shall be acquitted of
great transgression.
14 Let the words of my mouth
and the meditation of my
heart
Be acceptable in Your sight,
O LORD, my rock and my
Redeemer.

PSALM 20

Prayer for Victory over Enemies.
For the choir director.
A Psalm of David.

1 May the LORD answer you in
the day of trouble!
May the name of the God of
Jacob set you *securely* on
high!
2 May He send you help from
the sanctuary
And support you from Zion!
3 May He remember all your
meal offerings

And find your burnt offering
acceptable!   Selah.
4 May He grant you your heart's
desire
And fulfill all your ²counsel!
5 We will sing for joy over your
victory,
And in the name of our God
we will set up our banners.
May the LORD fulfill all your
petitions.
6 Now I know that the LORD
saves His anointed;
He will answer him from His
holy heaven
With the saving strength of
His right hand.
7 Some *boast* in chariots and
some in horses,
But we will boast in the name
of the LORD, our God.
8 They have bowed down and
fallen,
But we have risen and stood
upright.
9 Save, O LORD;
May the King answer us in the
day we call.

PSALM 21

Praise for Deliverance.
For the choir director.
A Psalm of David.

1 O LORD, in Your strength the
king will be glad,
And in Your ³salvation how
greatly he will rejoice!
2 You have given him his
heart's desire,
And You have not withheld
the request of his lips.   Selah.
3 For You meet him with the
blessings of good things;
You set a crown of fine gold
on his head.

1. Lit *complete* 2. Or *purpose* 3. Or *victory*

4 He asked life of You,
   You gave it to him,
   Length of days forever and
   ever.
5 His glory is great through
   Your ¹salvation,
   Splendor and majesty You
   place upon him.
6 For You make him most
   blessed forever;
   You make him joyful with
   gladness in Your presence.
7 For the king trusts in the
   LORD,
   And through the
   lovingkindness of the Most
   High he will not be shaken.
8 Your hand will find out all
   your enemies;
   Your right hand will find out
   those who hate you.
9 You will make them as a fiery
   oven in the time of your
   anger;
   The LORD will swallow them
   up in His wrath,
   And fire will devour them.
10 Their ²offspring You will
   destroy from the earth,
   And their ³descendants from
   among the sons of men.
11 Though they intended evil
   against You
   And devised a plot,
   They will not succeed.
12 For You will make them turn
   their back;
   You will aim with Your
   bowstrings at their faces.
13 Be exalted, O LORD, in Your
   strength;
   We will sing and praise Your
   power.

PSALM 22

*A Cry of Anguish and a
Song of Praise.*
For the choir director; upon
⁴Aijeleth Hashshahar.
A Psalm of David.

1 My God, my God, why have
   You forsaken me?
   Far from my deliverance are
   the words of my groaning.
2 O my God, I cry by day, but
   You do not answer;
   And by night, but I have no
   rest.
3 Yet You are holy,
   O You who are enthroned
   upon the praises of Israel.
4 In You our fathers trusted;
   They trusted and You
   delivered them.
5 To You they cried out and
   were delivered;
   In You they trusted and were
   not disappointed.
6 But I am a worm and not a
   man,
   A reproach of men and
   despised by the people.
7 All who see me sneer at me;
   They ⁵separate with the lip,
   they wag the head, *saying,*
8 "⁶Commit *yourself* to the LORD;
   let Him deliver him;
   Let Him rescue him, because
   He delights in him."
9 Yet You are He who brought
   me forth from the womb;
   You made me trust *when*
   upon my mother's breasts.
10 Upon You I was cast from
   birth;
   You have been my God from
   my mother's womb.

1. Or *victory* 2. Lit *fruit* 3. Lit *seed* 4. Lit *the hind of the morning* 5. I.e. make
mouths at me 6. Lit *Roll;* another reading is *He committed* himself

11 Be not far from me, for trouble
   is near;
   For there is none to help.
12 Many bulls have surrounded
   me;
   Strong *bulls* of Bashan have
   encircled me.
13 They open wide their mouth
   at me,
   As a ravening and a roaring
   lion.
14 I am poured out like water,
   And all my bones are out of
   joint;
   My heart is like wax;
   It is melted within me.
15 My strength is dried up like a
   potsherd,
   And my tongue cleaves to my
   jaws;
   And You lay me in the dust of
   death.
16 For dogs have surrounded me;
   A band of evildoers has
   encompassed me;
   They pierced my hands and
   my feet.
17 I can count all my bones.
   They look, they stare at me;
18 They divide my garments
   among them,
   And for my clothing they cast
   lots.
19 But You, O LORD, be not far
   off;
   O You my help, hasten to my
   assistance.
20 Deliver my soul from the
   sword,
   My only *life* from the power of
   the dog.
21 Save me from the lion's
   mouth;
   From the horns of the wild
   oxen You answer me.

22 I will tell of Your name to my
   brethren;
   In the midst of the assembly I
   will praise You.
23 You who fear the LORD, praise
   Him;
   All you descendants of Jacob,
   glorify Him,
   And stand in awe of Him, all
   you descendants of Israel.
24 For He has not despised nor
   abhorred the affliction of the
   afflicted;
   Nor has He hidden His face
   from him;
   But when he cried to Him for
   help, He heard.
25 From You *comes* my praise in
   the great assembly;
   I shall pay my vows before
   those who fear Him.
26 The ¹afflicted will eat and be
   satisfied;
   Those who seek Him will
   praise the LORD.
   Let your heart live forever!
27 All the ends of the earth will
   remember and turn to the
   LORD,
   And all the families of the
   nations will worship before
   You.
28 For the kingdom is the LORD'S
   And He rules over the nations.
29 All the prosperous of the earth
   will eat and worship,
   All those who go down to the
   dust will bow before Him,
   Even he who cannot keep his
   soul alive.
30 Posterity will serve Him;
   It will be told of the Lord to
   the *coming* generation.
31 They will come and will
   declare His righteousness

1. Or *poor*

To a people who will be born,
that He has performed *it*.

PSALM 23

*The LORD, the
Psalmist's Shepherd.*
A Psalm of David.

1 The LORD is my shepherd,
I shall not want.
2 He makes me lie down in
green pastures;
He leads me beside quiet
waters.
3 He restores my soul;
He guides me in the paths of
righteousness
For His name's sake.
4 Even though I walk through
the ¹valley of the shadow of
death,
I fear no ²evil, for You are
with me;
Your rod and Your staff, they
comfort me.
5 You prepare a table before me
in the presence of my
enemies;
You have anointed my head
with oil;
My cup overflows.
6 Surely goodness and
lovingkindness will follow me
all the days of my life,
And I will ³dwell in the house
of the LORD forever.

PSALM 24

The King of Glory Entering Zion.
A Psalm of David.

1 The earth is the LORD's, and
⁴all it contains,
The world, and those who
dwell in it.
2 For He has founded it upon
the seas

And established it upon the
rivers.
3 Who may ascend into the hill
of the LORD?
And who may stand in His
holy place?
4 He who has clean hands and a
pure heart,
Who has not lifted up his soul
to falsehood
And has not sworn deceitfully.
5 He shall receive a blessing
from the LORD
And righteousness from the
God of his salvation.
6 This is the generation of those
who seek Him,
Who seek Your face—*even*
Jacob.   Selah.
7 Lift up your heads, O gates,
And be lifted up, O ⁵ancient
doors,
That the King of glory may
come in!
8 Who is the King of glory?
The LORD strong and mighty,
The LORD mighty in battle.
9 Lift up your heads, O gates,
And lift *them* up, O ⁶ancient
doors,
That the King of glory may
come in!
10 Who is this King of glory?
The LORD of hosts,
He is the King of glory. Selah.

PSALM 25

*Prayer for Protection,
Guidance and Pardon.*
A Psalm of David.

1 To You, O LORD, I lift up my
soul.
2 O my God, in You I trust,
Do not let me be ashamed;

---
1. Or *valley of deep darkness* 2. Or *harm* 3. Another reading is *return to* 4. Lit *its
fullness* 5. Lit *everlasting* 6. Lit *everlasting*

19

Do not let my enemies exult
over me.
3 Indeed, none of those who
wait for You will be ashamed;
Those who deal treacherously
without cause will be
ashamed.
4 Make me know Your ways, O
Lord;
Teach me Your paths.
5 Lead me in Your truth and
teach me,
For You are the God of my
salvation;
For You I wait all the day.
6 Remember, O Lord, Your
compassion and Your
lovingkindnesses,
For they have been ¹from of
old.
7 Do not remember the sins of
my youth or my
transgressions;
According to Your
lovingkindness remember me,
For Your goodness' sake, O
Lord.
8 Good and upright is the Lord;
Therefore He instructs sinners
in the way.
9 He leads the humble in justice,
And He teaches the humble
His way.
10 All the paths of the Lord are
lovingkindness and truth
To those who keep His
covenant and His testimonies.
11 For Your name's sake, O
Lord,
Pardon my iniquity, for it is
great.
12 Who is the man who fears the
Lord?
He will instruct him in the
way he should choose.

13 His soul will abide in
prosperity,
And his ²descendants will
inherit the land.
14 The secret of the Lord is for
those who fear Him,
And He will make them know
His covenant.
15 My eyes are continually
toward the Lord,
For He will pluck my feet out
of the net.
16 Turn to me and be gracious to
me,
For I am lonely and afflicted.
17 The troubles of my heart are
enlarged;
Bring me out of my distresses.
18 Look upon my affliction and
my ³trouble,
And forgive all my sins.
19 Look upon my enemies, for
they are many,
And they hate me with violent
hatred.
20 Guard my soul and deliver
me;
Do not let me be ashamed, for
I take refuge in You.
21 Let integrity and uprightness
preserve me,
For I wait for You.
22 Redeem Israel, O God,
Out of all his troubles.

PSALM 26

*Protestation of Integrity and
Prayer for Protection.
A Psalm of David.*

1 ⁴Vindicate me, O Lord, for I
have walked in my integrity,
And I have trusted in the
Lord without wavering.

1. Or *everlasting* 2. Lit *seed* 3. Lit *toil* 4. Lit *Judge*

2 Examine me, O LORD, and try me;
Test my ¹mind and my heart.

3 For Your lovingkindness is before my eyes,
And I have walked in Your truth.

4 I do not sit with ²deceitful men,
Nor will I go with pretenders.

5 I hate the assembly of evildoers,
And I will not sit with the wicked.

6 I shall wash my hands in innocence,
And I will go about Your altar, O LORD,

7 That I may proclaim with the voice of thanksgiving
And declare all Your wonders.

8 O LORD, I love the habitation of Your house
And the place where Your glory dwells.

9 Do not take my soul away *along* with sinners,
Nor my life with men of bloodshed,

10 In whose hands is a wicked scheme,
And whose right hand is full of bribes.

11 But as for me, I shall walk in my integrity;
Redeem me, and be gracious to me.

12 My foot stands on a level place;
In the congregations I shall bless the LORD.

PSALM 27

*A Psalm of Fearless
Trust in God.
A Psalm* of David.

1 The LORD is my light and my salvation;
Whom shall I fear?
The LORD is the defense of my life;
Whom shall I dread?

2 When evildoers came upon me to devour my flesh,
My adversaries and my enemies, they stumbled and fell.

3 Though a host encamp against me,
My heart will not fear;
Though war arise against me,
In *spite of* this I shall be confident.

4 One thing I have asked from the LORD, that I shall seek:
That I may dwell in the house of the LORD all the days of my life,
To behold the ³beauty of the LORD
And to ⁴meditate in His temple.

5 For in the day of trouble He will conceal me in His tabernacle;
In the secret place of His tent He will hide me;
He will lift me up on a rock.

6 And now my head will be lifted up above my enemies around me,
And I will offer in His tent sacrifices with shouts of joy;
I will sing, yes, I will sing praises to the LORD.

1. Lit *kidneys*, figurative for inner man 2. Or *worthless men*; lit *men of falsehood*
3. Lit *delightfulness* 4. Lit *inquire*

7 Hear, O LORD, when I cry with
my voice,
And be gracious to me and
answer me.

8 *When You said,* "Seek My
face," my heart said to You,
"Your face, O LORD, I shall
seek."

9 Do not hide Your face from
me,
Do not turn Your servant
away in anger;
You have been my help;
Do not abandon me nor
forsake me,
O God of my salvation!

10 For my father and my mother
have forsaken me,
But the LORD will take me up.

11 Teach me Your way, O LORD,
And lead me in a level path
Because of my foes.

12 Do not deliver me over to the
desire of my adversaries,
For false witnesses have risen
against me,
And such as breathe out
violence.

13 *I would have despaired* unless I
had believed that I would see
the goodness of the LORD
In the land of the living.

14 Wait for the LORD;
Be strong and let your heart
take courage;
Yes, wait for the LORD.

PSALM 28

*A Prayer for Help, and
Praise for Its Answer.
A Psalm of David.*

1 To You, O LORD, I call;
My rock, do not be deaf to me,
For if You are silent to me,
I will become like those who
go down to the pit.

2 Hear the voice of my
supplications when I cry to
You for help,
When I lift up my hands
toward ¹Your holy sanctuary.

3 Do not drag me away with the
wicked
And with those who work
iniquity,
Who speak peace with their
neighbors,
While evil is in their hearts.

4 Requite them according to
their work and according to
the evil of their practices;
Requite them according to the
deeds of their hands;
Repay them their
²recompense.

5 Because they do not regard
the works of the LORD
Nor the deeds of His hands,
He will tear them down and
not build them up.

6 Blessed be the LORD,
Because He has heard the
voice of my supplication.

7 The LORD is my strength and
my shield;
My heart trusts in Him, and I
am helped;
Therefore my heart exults,
And with my song I shall
thank Him.

8 The LORD is their strength,
And He is a saving defense to
His anointed.

9 Save Your people and bless
Your inheritance;
Be their shepherd also, and
carry them forever.

1. Lit *the innermost place of Your sanctuary* 2. Or *dealings*

PSALM 29

*The Voice of the LORD
in the Storm.*
A Psalm of David.

1 Ascribe to the LORD, O sons of
the mighty,
Ascribe to the LORD glory and
strength.
2 Ascribe to the LORD the glory
due to His name;
Worship the LORD in holy
array.
3 The voice of the LORD is upon
the waters;
The God of glory thunders,
The LORD is over many waters.
4 The voice of the LORD is
powerful,
The voice of the LORD is
majestic.
5 The voice of the LORD breaks
the cedars;
Yes, the LORD breaks in pieces
the cedars of Lebanon.
6 He makes Lebanon skip like a
calf,
And Sirion like a young wild
ox.
7 The voice of the LORD hews
out flames of fire.
8 The voice of the LORD shakes
the wilderness;
The LORD shakes the
wilderness of Kadesh.
9 The voice of the LORD makes
the deer to calve
And strips the forests bare;
And in His temple everything
says, "Glory!"
10 The LORD sat *as* King at the
flood;
Yes, the LORD sits as King
forever.
11 The LORD will give strength to
His people;

The LORD will bless His people
with peace.

PSALM 30

*Thanksgiving for Deliverance
from Death.*
A Psalm; a Song at the
Dedication of the House.
A Psalm of David.

1 I will extol You, O LORD, for
You have lifted me up,
And have not let my enemies
rejoice over me.
2 O LORD my God,
I cried to You for help, and
You healed me.
3 O LORD, You have brought up
my soul from Sheol;
You have kept me alive, that I
would not go down to the pit.
4 Sing praise to the LORD, you
His godly ones,
And give thanks to His holy
name.
5 For His anger is but for a
moment,
His favor is for a lifetime;
Weeping may last for the
night,
But a shout of joy *comes* in the
morning.
6 Now as for me, I said in my
prosperity,
"I will never be moved."
7 O LORD, by Your favor You
have made my mountain to
stand strong;
You hid Your face, I was
dismayed.
8 To You, O LORD, I called,
And to the Lord I made
supplication:
9"What profit is there in my
blood, if I go down to the pit?
Will the dust praise You? Will
it declare Your faithfulness?

23

10 "Hear, O Lord, and be gracious
   to me;
   O Lord, be my helper."
11 You have turned for me my
   mourning into dancing;
   You have loosed my sackcloth
   and girded me with gladness,
12 That *my* soul may sing praise
   to You and not be silent.
   O Lord my God, I will give
   thanks to You forever.

PSALM 31

*A Psalm of Complaint
and of Praise.*
For the choir director.
A Psalm of David.

1 In You, O Lord, I have taken
   refuge;
   Let me never be ashamed;
   In Your righteousness deliver
   me.
2 Incline Your ear to me, rescue
   me quickly;
   Be to me a rock of strength,
   A stronghold to save me.
3 For You are my rock and my
   fortress;
   For Your name's sake You
   will lead me and guide me.
4 You will pull me out of the net
   which they have secretly laid
   for me,
   For You are my strength.
5 Into Your hand I commit my
   spirit;
   You have ransomed me, O
   Lord, God of truth.
6 I hate those who regard vain
   idols,
   But I trust in the Lord.
7 I will rejoice and be glad in
   Your lovingkindness,
   Because You have seen my
   affliction;
   You have known the troubles
   of my soul,

8 And You have not given me
   over into the hand of the
   enemy;
   You have set my feet in a large
   place.
9 Be gracious to me, O Lord, for
   I am in distress;
   My eye is wasted away from
   grief, my soul and my body
   also.
10 For my life is spent with
   sorrow
   And my years with sighing;
   My strength has failed because
   of my iniquity,
   And my body has wasted
   away.
11 Because of all my adversaries,
   I have become a reproach,
   Especially to my neighbors,
   And an object of dread to my
   acquaintances;
   Those who see me in the street
   flee from me.
12 I am forgotten as a dead man,
   out of mind;
   I am like a broken vessel.
13 For I have heard the slander
   of many,
   Terror is on every side;
   While they took counsel
   together against me,
   They schemed to take away
   my life.
14 But as for me, I trust in You,
   O Lord,
   I say, "You are my God."
15 My times are in Your hand;
   Deliver me from the hand of
   my enemies and from those
   who persecute me.
16 Make Your face to shine upon
   Your servant;
   Save me in Your
   lovingkindness.
17 Let me not be put to shame, O
   Lord, for I call upon You;

Let the wicked be put to
shame, let them be silent in
Sheol.
18 Let the lying lips be mute,
Which speak arrogantly
against the righteous
With pride and contempt.
19 How great is Your goodness,
Which You have stored up for
those who fear You,
Which You have wrought for
those who take refuge in You,
Before the sons of men!
20 You hide them in the secret
place of Your presence from
the conspiracies of man;
You keep them secretly in a
shelter from the strife of
tongues.
21 Blessed be the LORD,
For He has made marvelous
His lovingkindness to me in a
besieged city.
22 As for me, I said in my alarm,
"I am cut off from before Your
eyes";
Nevertheless You heard the
voice of my supplications
When I cried to You.
23 O love the LORD, all you His
godly ones!
The LORD preserves the
faithful
And fully recompenses the
proud doer.
24 Be strong and let your heart
take courage,
All you who hope in the LORD.

PSALM 32

*Blessedness of Forgiveness
and of Trust in God.*
A Psalm of David. A ¹Maskil.

1 How blessed is he whose
transgression is forgiven,

Whose sin is covered!
2 How blessed is the man to
whom the LORD does not
impute iniquity,
And in whose spirit there is no
deceit!
3 When I kept silent *about my
sin,* my body wasted away
Through my groaning all day
long.
4 For day and night Your hand
was heavy upon me;
My vitality was drained away
as with the fever heat of
summer.   Selah.
5 I acknowledged my sin to
You,
And my iniquity I did not
hide;
I said, "I will confess my
transgressions to the LORD";
And You forgave the guilt of
my sin.   Selah.
6 Therefore, let everyone who is
godly pray to You in a time
when You may be found;
Surely in a flood of great
waters they will not reach
him.
7 You are my hiding place; You
preserve me from trouble;
You surround me with songs
of deliverance.   Selah.
8 I will instruct you and teach
you in the way which you
should go;
I will counsel you with My eye
upon you.
9 Do not be as the horse or as
the mule which have no
understanding,
Whose trappings include bit
and bridle to hold them in
check,
Otherwise they will not come
near to you.

---

1. Possibly *Contemplative,* or *Didactic,* or *Skillful Psalm*

10 Many are the sorrows of the
   wicked,
   But he who trusts in the Lord,
   lovingkindness shall
   surround him.
11 Be glad in the Lord and
   rejoice, you righteous ones;
   And shout for joy, all you who
   are upright in heart.

PSALM 33

*Praise to the Creator
and Preserver.*

1 Sing for joy in the Lord, O you
   righteous ones;
   Praise is becoming to the
   upright.
2 Give thanks to the Lord with
   the lyre;
   Sing praises to Him with a
   harp of ten strings.
3 Sing to Him a new song;
   Play skillfully with a shout of
   joy.
4 For the word of the Lord is
   upright,
   And all His work is *done* in
   faithfulness.
5 He loves righteousness and
   justice;
   The earth is full of the
   lovingkindness of the Lord.
6 By the word of the Lord the
   heavens were made,
   And by the breath of His
   mouth all their host.
7 He gathers the waters of the
   sea together as a heap;
   He lays up the deeps in
   storehouses.
8 Let all the earth fear the Lord;
   Let all the inhabitants of the
   world stand in awe of Him.
9 For He spoke, and it was
   done;
   He commanded, and it stood
   fast.

10 The Lord nullifies the counsel
   of the nations;
   He frustrates the plans of the
   peoples.
11 The counsel of the Lord
   stands forever,
   The plans of His heart from
   generation to generation.
12 Blessed is the nation whose
   God is the Lord,
   The people whom He has
   chosen for His own
   inheritance.
13 The Lord looks from heaven;
   He sees all the sons of men;
14 From His dwelling place He
   looks out
   On all the inhabitants of the
   earth,
15 He who fashions the hearts of
   them all,
   He who understands all their
   works.
16 The king is not saved by a
   mighty army;
   A warrior is not delivered by
   great strength.
17 A horse is a false hope for
   victory;
   Nor does it deliver anyone by
   its great strength.
18 Behold, the eye of the Lord is
   on those who fear Him,
   On those who hope for His
   lovingkindness,
19 To deliver their soul from
   death
   And to keep them alive in
   famine.
20 Our soul waits for the Lord;
   He is our help and our shield.
21 For our heart rejoices in Him,
   Because we trust in His holy
   name.
22 Let Your lovingkindness, O
   Lord, be upon us,

According as we have hoped in You.

PSALM 34

The LORD, a Provider
and Deliverer.

A Psalm of David when he feigned madness before Abimelech, who drove him away and he departed.

1 I will bless the LORD at all times;
And His praise shall continually be in my mouth.

2 My soul will make its boast in the LORD;
The humble will hear it and rejoice.

3 O magnify the LORD with me,
And let us exalt His name together.

4 I sought the LORD, and He answered me,
And delivered me from all my fears.

5 They looked to Him and were radiant,
And their faces will never be ashamed.

6 This poor man cried, and the LORD heard him
And saved him out of all his troubles.

7 The angel of the LORD encamps around those who fear Him,
And rescues them.

8 O taste and see that the LORD is good;
How blessed is the man who takes refuge in Him!

9 O fear the LORD, you His saints;
For to those who fear Him there is no want.

10 The young lions do lack and suffer hunger;
But they who seek the LORD shall not be in want of any good thing.

11 Come, you children, listen to me;
I will teach you the fear of the LORD.

12 Who is the man who desires life
And loves *length of* days that he may see good?

13 Keep your tongue from evil
And your lips from speaking deceit.

14 Depart from evil and do good;
Seek peace and pursue it.

15 The eyes of the LORD are toward the righteous
And His ears are *open* to their cry.

16 The face of the LORD is against evildoers,
To cut off the memory of them from the earth.

17 *The righteous* cry, and the LORD hears
And delivers them out of all their troubles.

18 The LORD is near to the brokenhearted
And saves those who are ¹crushed in spirit.

19 Many are the afflictions of the righteous,
But the LORD delivers him out of them all.

20 He keeps all his bones,
Not one of them is broken.

21 Evil shall slay the wicked,
And those who hate the righteous will be condemned.

22 The LORD redeems the soul of His servants,
And none of those who take

1. Or *contrite*

refuge in Him will be condemned.

PSALM 35

Prayer for Rescue from Enemies.
A Psalm of David.

1 Contend, O LORD, with those
   who contend with me;
   Fight against those who fight
   against me.
2 Take hold of ¹buckler and
   shield
   And rise up for my help.
3 Draw also the spear and the
   battle-axe to meet those who
   pursue me;
   Say to my soul, "I am your
   salvation."
4 Let those be ashamed and
   dishonored who seek my life;
   Let those be turned back and
   humiliated who devise evil
   against me.
5 Let them be like chaff before
   the wind,
   With the angel of the LORD
   driving *them* on.
6 Let their way be dark and
   slippery,
   With the angel of the LORD
   pursuing them.
7 For without cause they hid
   their net for me;
   Without cause they dug a pit
   for my soul.
8 Let destruction come upon
   him unawares,
   And let the net which he hid
   catch himself;
   Into that very destruction let
   him fall.
9 And my soul shall rejoice in
   the LORD;
   It shall exult in His salvation.

10 All my bones will say, "LORD,
    who is like You,
    Who delivers the afflicted
    from him who is too strong
    for him,
    And the afflicted and the
    needy from him who robs
    him?"
11 Malicious witnesses rise up;
    They ask me of things that I
    do not know.
12 They repay me evil for good,
    To the bereavement of my
    soul.
13 But as for me, when they were
    sick, my clothing was
    sackcloth;
    I humbled my soul with
    fasting,
    And my prayer kept returning
    to my bosom.
14 I went about as though it were
    my friend or brother;
    I bowed down mourning, as
    one who sorrows for a
    mother.
15 But at my ²stumbling they
    rejoiced and gathered
    themselves together;
    The smiters whom I did not
    know gathered together
    against me,
    They slandered me without
    ceasing.
16 Like godless jesters at a feast,
    They gnashed at me with their
    teeth.
17 Lord, how long will You look
    on?
    Rescue my soul from their
    ravages,
    My only *life* from the lions.
18 I will give You thanks in the
    great congregation;
    I will praise You among a
    mighty throng.

---

1. I.e. small shield   2. Or *limping*

28

19 Do not let those who are
   wrongfully my enemies
   rejoice over me;
   Nor let those who hate me
   without cause wink
   maliciously.
20 For they do not speak peace,
   But they devise deceitful
   words against those who are
   quiet in the land.
21 They opened their mouth wide
   against me;
   They said, "Aha, aha, our eyes
   have seen it!"
22 You have seen it, O LORD, do
   not keep silent;
   O Lord, do not be far from me.
23 Stir up Yourself, and awake to
   my right
   And to my cause, my God and
   my Lord.
24 Judge me, O LORD my God,
   according to Your
   righteousness,
   And do not let them rejoice
   over me.
25 Do not let them say in their
   heart, "Aha, our desire!"
   Do not let them say, "We have
   swallowed him up!"
26 Let those be ashamed and
   humiliated altogether who
   rejoice at my distress;
   Let those be clothed with
   shame and dishonor who
   magnify themselves over me.
27 Let them shout for joy and
   rejoice, who favor my
   vindication;
   And let them say continually,
   "The LORD be magnified,
   Who delights in the prosperity
   of His servant."
28 And my tongue shall declare
   Your righteousness
   And Your praise all day long.

PSALM 36

*Wickedness of Men and
Lovingkindness of God.*

For the choir director. *A Psalm* of
David the servant of the LORD.

1 Transgression speaks to the
   ungodly within his heart;
   There is no fear of God before
   his eyes.
2 For it flatters him in his *own*
   eyes
   Concerning the discovery of
   his iniquity *and* the hatred *of
   it*.
3 The words of his mouth are
   wickedness and deceit;
   He has ceased to be wise *and*
   to do good.
4 He plans wickedness upon his
   bed;
   He sets himself on a path that
   is not good;
   He does not despise evil.
5 Your lovingkindness, O LORD,
   extends to the heavens,
   Your faithfulness *reaches* to
   the skies.
6 Your righteousness is like the
   mountains of God;
   Your judgments are *like* a
   great deep.
   O LORD, You preserve man
   and beast.
7 How precious is Your
   lovingkindness, O God!
   And the children of men take
   refuge in the shadow of Your
   wings.
8 They drink their fill of the
   abundance of Your house;
   And You give them to drink of
   the river of Your delights.
9 For with You is the fountain
   of life;
   In Your light we see light.
10 O continue Your

29

lovingkindness to those who
know You,
And Your righteousness to the
upright in heart.
11 Let not the foot of pride come
upon me,
And let not the hand of the
wicked drive me away.
12 There the doers of iniquity
have fallen;
They have been thrust down
and cannot rise.

PSALM 37

*Security of Those Who
Trust in the LORD, and
Insecurity of the Wicked.
A Psalm of David.*

1 Do not fret because of
evildoers,
Be not envious toward
wrongdoers.
2 For they will wither quickly
like the grass
And fade like the green herb.
3 Trust in the LORD and do
good;
Dwell in the land and
[1]cultivate faithfulness.
4 Delight yourself in the LORD;
And He will give you the
desires of your heart.
5 Commit your way to the
LORD,
Trust also in Him, and He will
do it.
6 He will bring forth your
righteousness as the light
And your judgment as the
noonday.
7 [2]Rest in the LORD and wait
[3]patiently for Him;
Do not fret because of him
who prospers in his way,

Because of the man who
carries out wicked schemes.
8 Cease from anger and forsake
wrath;
Do not fret; *it leads* only to
evildoing.
9 For evildoers will be cut off,
But those who wait for the
LORD, they will inherit the
land.
10 Yet a little while and the
wicked man will be no more;
And you will look carefully for
his place and he will not be
there.
11 But the humble will inherit the
land
And will delight themselves in
abundant prosperity.
12 The wicked plots against the
righteous
And gnashes at him with his
teeth.
13 The Lord laughs at him,
For He sees his day is coming.
14 The wicked have drawn the
sword and bent their bow
To cast down the afflicted and
the needy,
To slay those who are upright
in conduct.
15 Their sword will enter their
own heart,
And their bows will be broken.
16 Better is the little of the
righteous
Than the abundance of many
wicked.
17 For the arms of the wicked
will be broken,
But the LORD sustains the
righteous.
18 The LORD knows the days of
the blameless,
And their inheritance will be
forever.

---

1. Or *feed securely* or *feed on His faithfulness* 2. Or *Be still* 3. Or *longingly*

30

19 They will not be ashamed in
   the time of evil,
   And in the days of famine
   they will have abundance.
20 But the wicked will perish;
   And the enemies of the LORD
   will be like the ¹glory of the
   pastures,
   They vanish—like smoke they
   vanish away.
21 The wicked borrows and does
   not pay back,
   But the righteous is gracious
   and gives.
22 For those blessed by Him will
   inherit the land,
   But those cursed by Him will
   be cut off.
23 The steps of a man are
   established by the LORD,
   And He delights in his way.
24 When he falls, he will not be
   hurled headlong,
   Because the LORD is the One
   who holds his hand.
25 I have been young and now I
   am old,
   Yet I have not seen the
   righteous forsaken
   Or his descendants begging
   bread.
26 All day long he is gracious and
   lends,
   And his descendants are a
   blessing.
27 Depart from evil and do good,
   So you will abide forever.
28 For the LORD loves justice
   And does not forsake His
   godly ones;
   They are preserved forever,
   But the descendants of the
   wicked will be cut off.
29 The righteous will inherit the
   land
   And dwell in it forever.

30 The mouth of the righteous
   utters wisdom,
   And his tongue speaks justice.
31 The law of his God is in his
   heart;
   His steps do not slip.
32 The wicked spies upon the
   righteous
   And seeks to kill him.
33 The LORD will not leave him in
   his hand
   Or let him be condemned
   when he is judged.
34 Wait for the LORD and keep
   His way,
   And He will exalt you to
   inherit the land;
   When the wicked are cut off,
   you will see it.
35 I have seen a wicked, violent
   man
   Spreading himself like a
   luxuriant tree in its native
   soil.
36 Then he passed away, and lo,
   he was no more;
   I sought for him, but he could
   not be found.
37 Mark the blameless man, and
   behold the upright;
   For the man of peace will have
   a posterity.
38 But transgressors will be
   altogether destroyed;
   The posterity of the wicked
   will be cut off.
39 But the salvation of the
   righteous is from the LORD;
   He is their strength in time of
   trouble.
40 The LORD helps them and
   delivers them;
   He delivers them from the
   wicked and saves them,
   Because they take refuge in
   Him.

1. I.e. flowers

PSALM 38

Prayer of a Suffering Penitent.
A Psalm of David,
for a memorial.

1 O LORD, rebuke me not in
Your wrath,
And chasten me not in Your
burning anger.

2 For Your arrows have sunk
deep into me,
And Your hand has pressed
down on me.

3 There is no soundness in my
flesh because of Your
indignation;
There is no health in my bones
because of my sin.

4 For my iniquities are gone
over my head;
As a heavy burden they weigh
too much for me.

5 My wounds grow foul *and*
fester
Because of my folly.

6 I am bent over and greatly
bowed down;
I go mourning all day long.

7 For my loins are filled with
burning,
And there is no soundness in
my flesh.

8 I am benumbed and badly
crushed;
I groan because of the
agitation of my heart.

9 Lord, all my desire is before
You;
And my sighing is not hidden
from You.

10 My heart throbs, my strength
fails me;
And the light of my eyes, even
that has gone from me.

11 My loved ones and my friends
stand aloof from my plague;

And my kinsmen stand afar
off.

12 Those who seek my life lay
snares *for me;*
And those who seek to injure
me have threatened
destruction,
And they devise treachery all
day long.

13 But I, like a deaf man, do not
hear;
And *I am* like a mute man
who does not open his mouth.

14 Yes, I am like a man who does
not hear,
And in whose mouth are no
arguments.

15 For I hope in You, O LORD;
You will answer, O Lord my
God.

16 For I said, "May they not
rejoice over me,
Who, when my foot slips,
would magnify themselves
against me."

17 For I am ready to fall,
And my ¹sorrow is continually
before me.

18 For I confess my iniquity;
I am full of anxiety because of
my sin.

19 But my enemies are vigorous
and ²strong,
And many are those who hate
me wrongfully.

20 And those who repay evil for
good,
They oppose me, because I
follow what is good.

21 Do not forsake me, O LORD;
O my God, do not be far from
me!

22 Make haste to help me,
O Lord, my salvation!

1. Lit *pain* 2. Or *numerous*

PSALM 39

The Vanity of Life.
For the choir director, for
Jeduthun. A Psalm of David.

1 I said, "I will guard my ways
That I may not sin with my
tongue;
I will guard my mouth as with
a muzzle
While the wicked are in my
presence."

2 I was mute and silent,
I ¹refrained *even* from good,
And my ²sorrow grew worse.

3 My heart was hot within me,
While I was musing the fire
burned;
Then I spoke with my tongue:

4 "LORD, make me to know my
end
And what is the extent of my
days;
Let me know how transient I
am.

5 "Behold, You have made my
days *as* handbreadths,
And my lifetime as nothing in
Your sight;
Surely every man at his best is
a mere breath.   Selah.

6 "Surely every man walks about
as ³ªa phantom;
Surely they make an uproar
for nothing;
He amasses *riches* and does
not know who will gather
them.

7 "And now, Lord, for what do I
wait?
My hope is in You.

8 "Deliver me from all my
transgressions;
Make me not the reproach of
the foolish.

9 "I have become mute, I do not
open my mouth,
Because it is You who have
done *it.*

10 "Remove Your plague from
me;
Because of the opposition of
Your hand I am perishing.

11 "With reproofs You chasten a
man for iniquity;
You consume as a moth what
is precious to him;
Surely every man is a mere
breath.   Selah.

12 "Hear my prayer, O LORD, and
give ear to my cry;
Do not be silent at my tears;
For I am a stranger with You,
A sojourner like all my
fathers.

13 "Turn Your gaze away from
me, that I may ⁴smile *again*
Before I depart and am no
more."

PSALM 40

God Sustains His Servant.
For the choir director.
A Psalm of David.

1 I waited ⁵patiently for the
LORD;
And He inclined to me and
heard my cry.

2 He brought me up out of the
pit of destruction, out of the
miry clay,
And He set my feet upon a
rock making my footsteps
firm.

3 He put a new song in my
mouth, a song of praise to our
God;
Many will see and fear
And will trust in the LORD.

1. Lit *kept silence* 2. Lit *pain* 3. Lit *an image* 4. Or *become cheerful* 5. Or *intently*

4 How blessed is the man who
    has made the Lord his trust,
And has not turned to the
    proud, nor to those who lapse
    into falsehood.
5 Many, O Lord my God, are
    the wonders which You have
    done,
And Your thoughts toward us;
    There is none to compare with
    You.
If I would declare and speak
    of them,
They would be too numerous
    to count.
6 Sacrifice and meal offering
    You have not desired;
My ears You have ¹opened;
Burnt offering and sin offering
    You have not required.
7 Then I said, "Behold, I come;
In the scroll of the book it is
    written of me.
8 I delight to do Your will, O my
    God;
Your Law is within my heart."
9 I have proclaimed glad tidings
    of righteousness in the great
    congregation;
Behold, I will not restrain my
    lips,
O Lord, You know.
10 I have not hidden Your
    righteousness within my
    heart;
I have spoken of Your
    faithfulness and Your
    salvation;
I have not concealed Your
    lovingkindness and Your
    truth from the great
    congregation.
11 You, O Lord, will not
    withhold Your compassion
    from me;

Your lovingkindness and
    Your truth will continually
    preserve me.
12 For evils beyond number have
    surrounded me;
My iniquities have overtaken
    me, so that I am not able to
    see;
They are more numerous than
    the hairs of my head,
And my heart has failed me.
13 Be pleased, O Lord, to deliver
    me;
Make haste, O Lord, to help
    me.
14 Let those be ashamed and
    humiliated together
Who seek my ²life to destroy
    it;
Let those be turned back and
    dishonored
Who delight ³in my hurt.
15 Let those be appalled because
    of their shame
Who say to me, "Aha, aha!"
16 Let all who seek You rejoice
    and be glad in You;
Let those who love Your
    salvation say continually,
    "The Lord be magnified!"
17 Since I am afflicted and
    needy,
Let the Lord be mindful of me.
You are my help and my
    deliverer;
Do not delay, O my God.

PSALM 41

*The Psalmist in Sickness
Complains of Enemies
and False Friends.*
For the choir director.
A Psalm of David.

1 How blessed is he who
    considers the helpless;

1. Lit *dug;* or possibly *pierced* 2. Or *soul* 3. Or *to injure me*

34

The LORD will deliver him in a day of trouble.

2 The LORD will protect him and keep him alive,
And he shall be called blessed upon the earth;
And do not give him over to the desire of his enemies.

3 The LORD will sustain him upon his sickbed;
In his illness, You ¹restore him to health.

4 As for me, I said, "O LORD, be gracious to me;
Heal my soul, for I have sinned against You."

5 My enemies speak evil against me,
"When will he die, and his name perish?"

6 And when he comes to see *me*, he speaks falsehood;
His heart gathers wickedness to itself;
When he goes outside, he tells it.

7 All who hate me whisper together against me;
Against me they devise my hurt, *saying,*

8 "A wicked thing is poured out upon him,
That when he lies down, he will not rise up again."

9 Even my close friend in whom I trusted,
Who ate my bread,
Has lifted up his heel against me.

10 But You, O LORD, be gracious to me and raise me up,
That I may repay them.

11 By this I know that You are pleased with me,
Because my enemy does not shout in triumph over me.

12 As for me, You uphold me in my integrity,
And You set me in Your presence forever.

13 Blessed be the LORD, the God of Israel,
From everlasting to everlasting.
Amen and Amen.

BOOK 2
PSALM 42

Thirsting for God in Trouble and Exile.
For the choir director.
A Maskil of the sons of Korah.

1 As the deer ²pants for the water brooks,
So my soul pants for You, O God.

2 My soul thirsts for God, for the living God;
When shall I come and appear before God?

3 My tears have been my food day and night,
While *they* say to me all day long, "Where is your God?"

4 These things I remember and I pour out my soul within me.
For I used to go along with the throng *and* lead them in procession to the house of God,

With the voice of joy and thanksgiving, a multitude keeping festival.

5 Why are you in despair, O my soul?
And *why* have you become disturbed within me?

Hope in God, for I shall again praise Him

---

1. Lit *turn all his bed* 2. Lit *longs for*

35

For the help of His presence.

6 O my God, my soul is in
   despair within me;
   Therefore I remember You
   from the land of the Jordan
   And the peaks of Hermon,
   from Mount Mizar.

7 Deep calls to deep at the
   sound of Your waterfalls;
   All Your breakers and Your
   waves have rolled over me.

8 The LORD will command His
   lovingkindness in the
   daytime;
   And His song will be with me
   in the night,
   A prayer to the God of my life.

9 I will say to God my rock,
   "Why have You forgotten
   me?
   Why do I go mourning
   because of the oppression of
   the enemy?"

10 As a shattering of my bones,
   my adversaries revile me,
   While they say to me all day
   long, "Where is your God?"

11 Why are you in despair, O my
   soul?
   And why have you become
   disturbed within me?
   Hope in God, for I shall yet
   praise Him,
   The help of my countenance
   and my God.

PSALM 43

Prayer for Deliverance.

1 Vindicate me, O God, and
   plead my case against an
   ungodly nation;
   O deliver me from the
   deceitful and unjust man!

2 For You are the God of my
   strength; why have You
   rejected me?

Why do I go mourning
   because of the oppression of
   the enemy?

3 O send out Your light and
   Your truth, let them lead me;
   Let them bring me to Your
   holy hill
   And to Your dwelling places.

4 Then I will go to the altar of
   God,
   To God my exceeding joy;
   And upon the lyre I shall
   praise You, O God, my God.

5 Why are you in despair, O my
   soul?
   And why are you disturbed
   within me?
   Hope in God, for I shall again
   praise Him,
   The help of my countenance
   and my God.

PSALM 44

*Former Deliverances and
   Present Troubles.*
   For the choir director. A
   Maskil of the sons of Korah.

1 O God, we have heard with
   our ears,
   Our fathers have told us
   The work that You did in
   their days,
   In the days of old.

2 You with Your own hand
   drove out the nations;
   Then You planted them;
   You afflicted the peoples,
   Then You spread them
   abroad.

3 For by their own sword they
   did not possess the land,
   And their own arm did not
   save them,
   But Your right hand and Your
   arm and the light of Your
   presence,

For You favored them.

4 You are my King, O God;
Command victories for Jacob.

5 Through You we will push
back our adversaries;
Through Your name we will
trample down those who rise
up against us.

6 For I will not trust in my bow,
Nor will my sword save me.

7 But You have saved us from
our adversaries,
And You have put to shame
those who hate us.

8 In God we have boasted all
day long,
And we will give thanks to
Your name forever.   Selah.

9 Yet You have rejected *us* and
brought us to dishonor,
And do not go out with our
armies.

10 You cause us to turn back
from the adversary;
And those who hate us have
taken spoil for themselves.

11 You give us as sheep to be
eaten
And have scattered us among
the nations.

12 You sell Your people cheaply,
And have not ¹profited by
their sale.

13 You make us a reproach to
our neighbors,
A scoffing and a derision to
those around us.

14 You make us a byword among
the nations,
A laughingstock among the
peoples.

15 All day long my dishonor is
before me

And my humiliation has
overwhelmed me,

16 Because of the voice of him
who reproaches and reviles,
Because of the presence of the
enemy and the avenger.

17 All this has come upon us, but
we have not forgotten You,
And we have not dealt falsely
with Your covenant.

18 Our heart has not turned
back,
And our steps have not
deviated from Your way,

19 Yet You have crushed us in a
place of jackals
And covered us with the
shadow of death.

20 If we had forgotten the name
of our God
Or extended our hands to a
strange god,

21 Would not God find this out?
For He knows the secrets of
the heart.

22 But for Your sake we are
killed all day long;
We are considered as sheep to
be slaughtered.

23 Arouse Yourself, why do You
sleep, O Lord?
Awake, do not reject us
forever.

24 Why do You hide Your face
And forget our affliction and
our oppression?

25 For our soul has sunk down
into the dust;
Our body cleaves to the earth.

26 Rise up, be our help,
And redeem us for the sake of
Your lovingkindness.

1. Or *set a high price on them*

PSALM 45

*A Song Celebrating
the King's Marriage.*
For the choir director;
according to the [1]Shoshannim.
A Maskil of the sons of Korah.
A Song of Love.

1 My heart [2]overflows with a
  good theme;
  I address my verses to the
  King;
  My tongue is the pen of a
  ready writer.

2 You are fairer than the sons of
  men;
  Grace is poured upon Your
  lips;
  Therefore God has blessed
  You forever.

3 Gird Your sword on *Your*
  thigh, O Mighty One,
  In Your splendor and Your
  majesty!

4 And in Your majesty ride on
  victoriously,
  For the cause of truth and
  meekness *and* righteousness;
  Let Your right hand teach
  You awesome things.

5 Your arrows are sharp;
  The peoples fall under You;
  Your arrows are in the heart of
  the King's enemies.

6 Your throne, O God, is forever
  and ever;
  A scepter of uprightness is the
  scepter of Your kingdom.

7 You have loved righteousness
  and hated wickedness;
  Therefore God, Your God, has
  anointed You
  With the oil of joy above Your
  fellows.

8 All Your garments are
fragrant with myrrh and aloes
  and cassia;
  Out of ivory palaces stringed
  instruments have made You
  glad.

9 Kings' daughters are among
  Your noble ladies;
  At Your right hand stands the
  queen in gold from Ophir.

10 Listen, O daughter, give
   attention and incline your
   ear:
   Forget your people and your
   father's house;

11 Then the King will desire your
   beauty.
   Because He is your Lord, bow
   down to Him.

12 The daughter of Tyre *will
   come* with a gift;
   The rich among the people
   will seek your favor.

13 The King's daughter is all
   glorious within;
   Her clothing is interwoven
   with gold.

14 She will be led to the King in
   embroidered work;
   The virgins, her companions
   who follow her,
   Will be brought to You.

15 They will be led forth with
   gladness and rejoicing;
   They will enter into the King's
   palace.

16 In place of your fathers will be
   your sons;
   You shall make them princes
   in all the earth.

17 I will cause Your name to be
   remembered in all
   generations;
   Therefore the peoples will give
   You thanks forever and ever.

1. Or possibly *Lilies* 2. Lit *is astir*

38

PSALM 46

God the Refuge of His People.
For the choir director. *A Psalm*
of the sons of Korah, [1]set to
Alamoth. A Song.

1 God is our refuge and
   strength,
   [2]A very present help in
   trouble.
2 Therefore we will not fear,
   though the earth should
   change
   And though the mountains
   slip into the heart of the sea;
3 Though its waters roar *and*
   foam,
   Though the mountains quake
   at its swelling pride.   Selah.
4 There is a river whose streams
   make glad the city of God,
   The holy dwelling places of
   the Most High.
5 God is in the midst of her, she
   will not be moved;
   God will help her when
   morning dawns.
6 The nations made an uproar,
   the kingdoms tottered;
   He raised His voice, the earth
   melted.
7 The LORD of hosts is with us;
   The God of Jacob is our
   stronghold.   Selah.
8 Come, behold the works of the
   LORD,
   Who has wrought desolations
   in the earth.
9 He makes wars to cease to the
   end of the earth;
   He breaks the bow and cuts
   the spear in two;
   He burns the chariots with
   fire.
10 "Cease *striving* and know that I
   am God;

I will be exalted among the
   nations, I will be exalted in
   the earth."
11 The LORD of hosts is with us;
   The God of Jacob is our
   stronghold.   Selah.

PSALM 47

God the King of the Earth.
For the choir director. A Psalm
   of the sons of Korah.

1 O clap your hands, all peoples;
   Shout to God with the voice of
   joy.
2 For the LORD Most High is to
   be feared,
   A great King over all the
   earth.
3 He subdues peoples under us
   And nations under our feet.
4 He chooses our inheritance for
   us,
   The glory of Jacob whom He
   loves.   Selah.
5 God has ascended with a
   shout,
   The LORD, with the sound of a
   trumpet.
6 Sing praises to God, sing
   praises;
   Sing praises to our King, sing
   praises.
7 For God is the King of all the
   earth;
   Sing praises with a skillful
   psalm.
8 God reigns over the nations,
   God sits on His holy throne.
9 The princes of the people have
   assembled themselves *as* the
   people of the God of
   Abraham,
   For the shields of the earth
   belong to God;
   He is highly exalted.

---

1. Possibly *for soprano voices* 2. Or *Abundantly available for help*

PSALM 48

The Beauty and Glory of Zion.
A Song; a Psalm of the sons
of Korah.

1 Great is the Lord, and greatly
to be praised,
In the city of our God, His
holy mountain.

2 Beautiful in elevation, the joy
of the whole earth,
Is Mount Zion *in* the far
north,
The city of the great King.

3 God, in her palaces,
Has made Himself known as a
stronghold.

4 For, lo, the kings assembled
themselves,
They passed by together.

5 They saw *it*, then they were
amazed;
They were terrified, they fled
in alarm.

6 Panic seized them there,
Anguish, as of a woman in
childbirth.

7 With the east wind
You break the ships of
Tarshish.

8 As we have heard, so have we
seen
In the city of the Lord of
hosts, in the city of our God;
God will establish her forever.
Selah.

9 We have thought on Your
lovingkindness, O God,
In the midst of Your temple.

10 As is Your name, O God,
So is Your praise to the ends
of the earth;
Your right hand is full of
righteousness.

11 Let Mount Zion be glad,

Let the daughters of Judah
rejoice
Because of Your judgments.

12 Walk about Zion and go
around her;
Count her towers;

13 Consider her ramparts;
Go through her palaces,
That you may tell *it* to the
next generation.

14 For such is God,
Our God forever and ever;
He will guide us [1]until death.

PSALM 49

The Folly of Trusting in Riches.
For the choir director.
A Psalm of the sons of Korah.

1 Hear this, all peoples;
Give ear, all inhabitants of the
world,

2 Both low and high,
Rich and poor together.

3 My mouth will speak wisdom,
And the meditation of my
heart *will be* understanding.

4 I will incline my ear to a
proverb;
I will express my riddle on the
harp.

5 Why should I fear in days of
adversity,
When the iniquity of my foes
surrounds me,

6 Even those who trust in their
wealth
And boast in the abundance of
their riches?

7 No man can by any means
redeem *his* brother
Or give to God a ransom for
him—

8 For the redemption of his soul
is costly,

1. Lit *upon;* some mss and the Gr read *forever*

40

And he should cease *trying*
forever—

9 That he should live on
eternally,
That he should not [1]undergo
decay.

10 For he sees *that even* wise men
die;
The stupid and the senseless
alike perish
And leave their wealth to
others.

11 Their [2]inner thought is *that*
their houses are forever
And their dwelling places to
all generations;
They have called their lands
after their own names.

12 But man in *his* pomp will not
endure;
He is like the beasts that
perish.

13 This is the way of those who
are foolish,
And of those after them who
approve their words.   Selah.

14 As sheep they are appointed
for Sheol;
Death shall be their shepherd;
And the upright shall rule
over them in the morning,
And their form shall be for
Sheol to consume
So that they have no
habitation.

15 But God will redeem my soul
from the power of Sheol,
For He will receive me.   Selah.

16 Do not be afraid when a man
becomes rich,
When the [3]glory of his house is
increased;

17 For when he dies he will carry
nothing away;

His [4]glory will not descend
after him.

18 Though while he lives he
congratulates himself—
And though *men* praise you
when you do well for
yourself—

19 He shall go to the generation
of his fathers;
They will never see the light.

20 Man in *his* pomp, yet without
understanding,
Is like the beasts that perish.

PSALM 50

God the Judge of the
Righteous and the Wicked.
A Psalm of Asaph.

1 The Mighty One, God, the
LORD, has spoken,
And summoned the earth
from the rising of the sun to
its setting.

2 Out of Zion, the perfection of
beauty,
God has shone forth.

3 May our God come and not
keep silence;
Fire devours before Him,
And it is very tempestuous
around Him.

4 He summons the heavens
above,
And the earth, to judge His
people:

5 "Gather My godly ones to Me,
Those who have made a
covenant with Me by
sacrifice."

6 And the heavens declare His
righteousness,
For God Himself is judge.
Selah.

7 "Hear, O My people, and I will
speak;

1. Or *see corruption* or *the pit* 2. Some versions read *graves are their houses*
3. Or *wealth* 4. Or *wealth*

O Israel, I will testify against
  you;
I am God, your God.
8"I do not reprove you for your
  sacrifices,
And your burnt offerings are
  continually before Me.
9"I shall take no young bull out
  of your house
Nor male goats out of your
  folds.
10"For every beast of the forest is
  Mine,
The cattle on a thousand hills.
11"I know every bird of the
  mountains,
And everything that moves in
  the field is ¹Mine.
12"If I were hungry I would not
  tell you,
For the world is Mine, and all
  it contains.
13"Shall I eat the flesh of bulls
Or drink the blood of male
  goats?
14"Offer to God a sacrifice of
  thanksgiving
And pay your vows to the
  Most High;
15 Call upon Me in the day of
  trouble;
I shall rescue you, and you
  will honor Me."

16 But to the wicked God says,
  "What right have you to tell of
  My statutes
And to take My covenant in
  your mouth?
17"For you hate discipline,
And you cast My words
  behind you.
18"When you see a thief, you are
  pleased with him,
And you associate with
  adulterers.

19"You let your mouth loose in
  evil
And your tongue frames
  deceit.
20"You sit and speak against
  your brother;
You slander your own
  mother's son.
21"These things you have done
  and I kept silence;
You thought that I was just
  like you;
I will reprove you and state
  the case in order before your
  eyes.
22"Now consider this, you who
  forget God,
Or I will tear *you* in pieces,
  and there will be none to
  deliver.
23"He who offers a sacrifice of
  thanksgiving honors Me;
And to him who orders *his*
  way *aright*
I shall show the salvation of
  God."

PSALM 51

*A Contrite Sinner's Prayer
  for Pardon.*
For the choir director.
A Psalm of David, when Nathan
the prophet came to him, after
he had gone in to Bathsheba.

1 Be gracious to me, O God,
  according to Your
  lovingkindness;
According to the greatness of
  Your compassion blot out my
  transgressions.
2 Wash me thoroughly from my
  iniquity
And cleanse me from my sin.
3 For I know my transgressions,
  And my sin is ever before me.

1. Or *in My mind*; lit *with Me*

4 Against You, You only, I have
    sinned
    And done what is evil in Your
    sight,
    So that You ¹are justified
    when You speak
    And blameless when You
    judge.

5 Behold, I was brought forth in
    iniquity,
    And in sin my mother
    conceived me.

6 Behold, You desire truth in
    the innermost being,
    And in the hidden part You
    will make me know wisdom.

7 Purify me with hyssop, and I
    shall be clean;
    Wash me, and I shall be
    whiter than snow.

8 Make me to hear joy and
    gladness,
    Let the bones which You have
    broken rejoice.

9 Hide Your face from my sins
    And blot out all my iniquities.

10 Create in me a clean heart, O
    God,
    And renew a steadfast spirit
    within me.

11 Do not cast me away from
    Your presence
    And do not take Your Holy
    Spirit from me.

12 Restore to me the joy of Your
    salvation
    And sustain me with a willing
    spirit.

13 *Then* I will teach transgressors
    Your ways,
    And sinners will ²be converted
    to You.

14 Deliver me from
    bloodguiltiness, O God, the
    God of my salvation;

Then my tongue will joyfully
    sing of Your righteousness.

15 O Lord, open my lips,
    That my mouth may declare
    Your praise.

16 For You do not delight in
    sacrifice, otherwise I would
    give it;
    You are not pleased with
    burnt offering.

17 The sacrifices of God are a
    broken spirit;
    A broken and a contrite heart,
    O God, You will not despise.

18 By Your favor do good to
    Zion;
    Build the walls of Jerusalem.

19 Then You will delight in
    righteous sacrifices,
    In burnt offering and whole
    burnt offering;
    Then young bulls will be
    offered on Your altar.

PSALM 52

Futility of Boastful Wickedness.
    For the choir director.
A Maskil of David, when Doeg
the Edomite came and told Saul
and said to him, "David has
come to the house of Ahimelech."

1 Why do you boast in evil, O
    mighty man?
    The lovingkindness of God
    endures all day long.

2 Your tongue devises
    destruction,
    Like a sharp razor, O worker
    of deceit.

3 You love evil more than good,
    Falsehood more than speaking
    what is right.   Selah.

4 You love all words that
    devour,
    O deceitful tongue.

---

1. Or *may be in the right* 2. Or *turn back*

43

5 But God will break you down
forever;
He will snatch you up and tear
you away from *your* tent,
And uproot you from the land
of the living.   Selah.

6 The righteous will see and
fear,
And will laugh at him, *saying,*

7 "Behold, the man who would
not make God his refuge,
But trusted in the abundance
of his riches
And was strong in his *evil*
desire."

8 But as for me, I am like a
green olive tree in the house
of God;
I trust in the lovingkindness of
God forever and ever.

9 I will give You thanks forever,
because You have done *it,*
And I will wait on Your name,
for *it is* good, in the presence
of Your godly ones.

PSALM 53

Folly and Wickedness of Men.
For the choir director; according
to ¹Mahalath. A Maskil of David.

1 The fool has said in his heart,
"There is no God,"
They are corrupt, and have
committed abominable
injustice;
There is no one who does
good.

2 God has looked down from
heaven upon the sons of men
To see if there is anyone who
understands,
Who seeks after God.

3 Every one of them has turned
aside; together they have
become corrupt;

There is no one who does
good, not even one.

4 Have the workers of
wickedness no knowledge,
Who eat up My people *as
though* they ate bread
And have not called upon
God?

5 There they were in great fear
where no fear had been;
For God scattered the bones of
him who encamped against
you;
You put *them* to shame,
because God had rejected
them.

6 Oh, that the salvation of Israel
would come out of Zion!
When God restores His
captive people,
Let Jacob rejoice, let Israel be
glad.

PSALM 54

*Prayer for Defense
against Enemies.*
For the choir director; on stringed
instruments. A Maskil of David,
when the Ziphites came and said
to Saul, "Is not David hiding
himself among us?"

1 Save me, O God, by Your
name,
And ²vindicate me by Your
power.

2 Hear my prayer, O God;
Give ear to the words of my
mouth.

3 For strangers have risen
against me
And violent men have sought
my life;
They have not set God before
them.   Selah.

4 Behold, God is my helper;

---

1. I.e. sickness, a sad tone 2. Lit *judge*

The Lord is the sustainer of
my soul.
5 [1]He will recompense the evil to
my foes;
Destroy them in Your
faithfulness.
6 Willingly I will sacrifice to
You;
I will give thanks to Your
name, O LORD, for it is good.
7 For He has delivered me from
all trouble,
And my eye has looked *with
satisfaction* upon my
enemies.

PSALM 55

*Prayer for the Destruction
of the Treacherous.*

For the choir director; on stringed
instruments. A Maskil of David.

1 Give ear to my prayer, O God;
And do not hide Yourself from
my supplication.
2 Give heed to me and answer
me;
I am restless in my complaint
and [2]am surely distracted,
3 Because of the voice of the
enemy,
Because of the pressure of the
wicked;
For they bring down trouble
upon me
And in anger they bear a
grudge against me.
4 My heart is in anguish within
me,
And the terrors of death have
fallen upon me.
5 Fear and trembling come
upon me,
And horror has overwhelmed
me.

6 I said, "Oh, that I had wings
like a dove!
I would fly away and [3]be at
rest.
7 "Behold, I would wander far
away,
I would lodge in the
wilderness.   Selah.
8 "I would hasten to my place of
refuge
From the stormy wind *and*
tempest."

9 Confuse, O Lord, divide their
tongues,
For I have seen violence and
strife in the city.
10 Day and night they go around
her upon her walls,
And iniquity and mischief are
in her midst.
11 Destruction is in her midst;
Oppression and deceit do not
depart from her streets.
12 For it is not an enemy who
reproaches me,
Then I could bear *it;*
Nor is it one who hates me
who has exalted himself
against me,
Then I could hide myself from
him.
13 But it is you, a man my equal,
My companion and my
familiar friend;
14 We who had sweet [4]fellowship
together
Walked in the house of God in
the throng.
15 Let death come deceitfully
upon them;
Let them go down alive to
Sheol,

1. Lit *The evil will return* 2. Or *I must moan* 3. Lit *settle down* 4. Lit *counsel;* or
intimacy

45

For evil is in their dwelling, in their midst.

16 As for me, I shall call upon God,
And the LORD will save me.

17 Evening and morning and at noon, I will complain and murmur,
And He will hear my voice.

18 He will redeem my soul in peace from the battle *which is* against me,
For they are many *who strive* with me.

19 God will hear and answer them—
Even the one who sits enthroned from of old—

Selah.

With whom there is no change,
And who do not fear God.

20 He has put forth his hands against those who were at peace with him;
He has ¹violated his covenant.

21 His speech was smoother than butter,
But his heart was war;
His words were softer than oil,
Yet they were drawn swords.

22 Cast your burden upon the LORD and He will sustain you;
He will never allow the righteous to be shaken.

23 But You, O God, will bring them down to the pit of destruction;
Men of bloodshed and deceit will not live out half their days.
But I will trust in You.

PSALM 56

Supplication for Deliverance and Grateful Trust in God.

For the choir director; according to Jonath elem rehokim. A Mikhtam of David, when the Philistines seized him in Gath.

1 Be gracious to me, O God, for man has trampled upon me;
Fighting all day long he oppresses me.

2 My foes have trampled upon me all day long,
For they are many who fight proudly against me.

3 When I am afraid,
I will put my trust in You.

4 In God, whose word I praise,
In God I have put my trust;
I shall not be afraid.
What can *mere* man do to me?

5 All day long they ²distort my words;
All their thoughts are against me for evil.

6 They ³attack, they lurk,
They watch my steps,
As they have waited *to take* my life.

7 Because of wickedness, cast them forth,
In anger put down the peoples, O God!

8 You have taken account of my wanderings;
Put my tears in Your bottle.
Are *they* not in Your book?

9 Then my enemies will turn back in the day when I call;
This I know, ⁴that God is for me.

10 In God, *whose* word I praise,
In the LORD, *whose* word I praise,

---

1. Lit *profaned*   2. Or *trouble my affairs*   3. Or *stir up strife*   4. Or *because*

11 In God I have put my ¹trust, I
   shall not be afraid.
   What can man do to me?
12 Your vows are *binding* upon
   me, O God;
   I will render thank offerings to
   You.
13 For You have delivered my
   soul from death,
   Indeed my feet from
   stumbling,
   So that I may walk before God
   In the light of the living.

PSALM 57

*Prayer for Rescue
from Persecutors.*
For the choir director; *set to*
²Al-tashheth. A Mikhtam of
David, when he fled from
Saul in the cave.

1 Be gracious to me, O God, be
   gracious to me,
   For my soul takes refuge in
   You;

   And in the shadow of Your
   wings I will take refuge

   Until destruction passes by.
2 I will cry to God Most High,
   To God who accomplishes *all
   things* for me.
3 He will send from heaven and
   save me;
   He reproaches him who
   tramples upon me.   Selah.

   God will send forth His
   lovingkindness and His truth.

4 My soul is among lions;
   I must lie among those who
   breathe forth fire,

   Even the sons of men, whose
   teeth are spears and arrows

And their tongue a sharp
   sword.
5 Be exalted above the heavens,
   O God;
   Let Your glory *be* above all the
   earth.
6 They have ³prepared a net for
   my steps;
   My soul is bowed down;
   They dug a pit before me;
   They *themselves* have fallen
   into the midst of it.   Selah.
7 My heart is steadfast, O God,
   my heart is steadfast;
   I will sing, yes, I will sing
   praises!
8 Awake, my glory!
   Awake, harp and lyre!
   I will awaken the dawn.
9 I will give thanks to You, O
   Lord, among the peoples;
   I will sing praises to You
   among the nations.
10 For Your lovingkindness is
   great to the heavens
   And Your truth to the clouds.
11 Be exalted above the heavens,
   O God;
   Let Your glory *be* above all the
   earth.

PSALM 58

*Prayer for the Punishment
of the Wicked.*
For the choir director; *set to*
Al-tashheth. A Mikhtam
of David.

1 Do you indeed speak
   righteousness, O ⁴gods?
   Do you judge ⁵uprightly, O
   sons of men?
2 No, in heart you work
   unrighteousness;

---

1. Or *trust without fear* 2. Lit *Do Not Destroy* 3. Or *spread* 4. Or *mighty ones* or *judges* 5. Or *uprightly the sons of men*

47

On earth you weigh out the
violence of your hands.

3 The wicked are estranged
from the womb;
These who speak lies go astray
from birth.

4 They have venom like the
venom of a serpent;
Like a deaf cobra that stops
up its ear,

5 So that it does not hear the
voice of charmers,
Or a skillful caster of
spells.

6 O God, shatter their teeth in
their mouth;
Break out the fangs of the
young lions, O LORD.

7 Let them flow away like water
that runs off;
When he aims his arrows,
let them be as headless
shafts.

8 *Let them be* as a snail which
melts away as it goes along,
Like the miscarriages of a
woman which never see the
sun.

9 Before your pots can feel *the
fire of* thorns
He will sweep them away with
a whirlwind, the green and
the burning alike.

10 The righteous will rejoice
when he sees the
vengeance;
He will wash his feet in the
blood of the wicked.

11 And men will say, "Surely
there is a reward for the
righteous;
Surely there is a God who
judges on earth!"

1. Or *stir up strife*

PSALM 59

*Prayer for Deliverance
from Enemies.*
For the choir director; *set to*
Al-tashheth. A Mikhtam of
David, when Saul sent *men* and
they watched the house in order
to kill him.

1 Deliver me from my enemies,
O my God;
Set me *securely* on high away
from those who rise up
against me.

2 Deliver me from those who do
iniquity
And save me from men of
bloodshed.

3 For behold, they have set an
ambush for my life;
Fierce men ¹launch an attack
against me,
Not for my transgression nor
for my sin, O LORD,

4 For no guilt of *mine*, they run
and set themselves against
me.
Arouse Yourself to help me,
and see!

5 You, O LORD God of hosts, the
God of Israel,
Awake to punish all the
nations;
Do not be gracious to any *who
are* treacherous in iniquity.
Selah.

6 They return at evening, they
howl like a dog,
And go around the city.

7 Behold, they belch forth with
their mouth;
Swords are in their lips,
For, *they say*, "Who hears?"

8 But You, O LORD, laugh at
them;
You scoff at all the nations.

48

9 *Because of* [1]his strength I will
watch for You,
For God is my stronghold.

10 My God in His lovingkindness
will meet me;
God will let me look
triumphantly upon my foes.

11 Do not slay them, or my
people will forget;
Scatter them by Your power,
and bring them down,
O Lord, our shield.

12 *On account of* the sin of their
mouth *and* the words of their
lips,
Let them even be caught in
their pride,
And on account of curses and
lies which they utter.

13 [2]Destroy *them* in wrath,
[2]destroy *them* that they may
be no more;
That *men* may know that God
rules in Jacob
To the ends of the earth.
Selah.

14 They return at evening, they
howl like a dog,
And go around the city.

15 They wander about [3]for food
And growl if they are not
satisfied.

16 But as for me, I shall sing of
Your strength;
Yes, I shall joyfully sing of
Your lovingkindness in the
morning,
For You have been my
stronghold
And a refuge in the day of my
distress.

17 O my strength, I will sing
praises to You;
For God is my stronghold, the

God who shows me
lovingkindness.

PSALM 60

*Lament over Defeat in
Battle, and Prayer for Help.*
For the choir director; according
to [4]Shushan Eduth. A Mikhtam
of David, to teach; when he
struggled with Aram-naharaim
and with Aram-zobah, and
Joab returned, and smote
twelve thousand of Edom in
the Valley of Salt.

1 O God, You have rejected us.
You have broken us;
You have been angry; O,
restore us.

2 You have made the land
quake, You have split it open;
Heal its breaches, for it totters.

3 You have made Your people
experience hardship;
You have given us wine to
drink that makes us stagger.

4 You have given a banner to
those who fear You,
That it may be displayed
because of the truth.   Selah.

5 That Your beloved may be
delivered,
Save with Your right hand,
and answer us!

6 God has spoken in His
[5]holiness:
"I will exult, I will portion out
Shechem and measure out
the valley of Succoth.

7"Gilead is Mine, and Manasseh
is Mine;
Ephraim also is the helmet of
My head;
Judah is My [6]scepter.

8"Moab is My washbowl;

---
1. Many mss and some ancient versions read *My strength* 2. Lit *Bring to an end*
3. Or *to devour* 4. Lit *The lily of testimony* 5. Or *sanctuary* 6. Or *lawgiver*

Over Edom I shall throw My
shoe;
Shout loud, O Philistia,
because of Me!"

9 Who will bring me into the
besieged city?
Who will lead me to Edom?

10 Have not You Yourself, O
God, rejected us?
And will You not go forth
with our armies, O God?

11 O give us help against the
adversary,
For deliverance by man is in
vain.

12 Through God we shall do
valiantly,
And it is He who will tread
down our adversaries.

PSALM 61

Confidence in God's Protection.
For the choir director; on a
stringed instrument.
A Psalm of David.

1 Hear my cry, O God;
Give heed to my prayer.

2 From the end of the earth I
call to You when my heart is
faint;
Lead me to the rock that is
higher than I.

3 For You have been a refuge
for me,
A tower of strength against
the enemy.

4 Let me dwell in Your tent
forever;
Let me take refuge in the
shelter of Your wings.   Selah.

5 For You have·heard my vows,
O God;
You have given *me* the
inheritance of those who fear
Your name.

6 You will prolong the king's
life;
His years will be as many
generations.

7 He will abide before God
forever;
Appoint lovingkindness and
truth that they may preserve
him.

8 So I will sing praise to Your
name forever,
That I may pay my vows day
by day.

PSALM 62

*God Alone a Refuge from
Treachery and Oppression.*
For the choir director; according
to Jeduthun. A Psalm of David.

1 My soul *waits* in silence for
God only;
From Him is my salvation.

2 He only is my rock and my
salvation,
My stronghold; I shall not be
greatly shaken.

3 How long will you assail a
man,
That you may murder *him,* all
of you,
Like a leaning wall, like a
tottering fence?

4 They have counseled only to
thrust him down from his
high position;
They delight in falsehood;
They bless with their mouth,
But inwardly they curse.
Selah.

5 My soul, wait in silence for
God only,
For my hope is from Him.

6 He only is my rock and my
salvation,
My stronghold; I shall not be
shaken.

7 On God my salvation and my
glory *rest;*
The rock of my strength, my
refuge is in God.
8 Trust in Him at all times, O
people;
Pour out your heart before
Him;
God is a refuge for us.   Selah.
9 Men of low degree are only
vanity and men of rank are a
lie;
In the balances they go up;
They are together lighter than
breath.
10 Do not trust in oppression
And do not vainly hope in
robbery;
If riches increase, do not set
your heart *upon them.*
11 ¹Once God has spoken;
²Twice I have heard this:
That power belongs to God;
12 And lovingkindness is Yours,
O Lord,
For You recompense a man
according to his work.

PSALM 63

*The Thirsting Soul
Satisfied in God.*
A Psalm of David, when he was
in the wilderness of Judah.

1 O God, You are my God; I
shall seek You ³earnestly;
My soul thirsts for You, my
flesh yearns for You,
In a dry and weary land where
there is no water.
2 Thus I have seen You in the
sanctuary,
To see Your power and Your
glory.
3 Because Your lovingkindness
is better than life,
My lips will praise You.
4 So I will bless You as long as I
live;
I will lift up my hands in Your
name.
5 My soul is satisfied as with
⁴marrow and fatness,
And my mouth offers praises
with joyful lips.
6 When I remember You on my
bed,
I meditate on You in the night
watches,
7 For You have been my help,
And in the shadow of Your
wings I sing for joy.
8 My soul clings to You;
Your right hand upholds me.
9 But those who seek my life to
destroy it,
Will go into the depths of the
earth.
10 They will be delivered over to
the power of the sword;
They will be a prey for foxes.
11 But the king will rejoice in
God;
Everyone who swears by Him
will glory,
For the mouths of those who
speak lies will be stopped.

PSALM 64

*Prayer for Deliverance from
Secret Enemies.*
For the choir director.
A Psalm of David.

1 Hear my voice, O God, in my
⁵complaint;
Preserve my life from dread of
the enemy.
2 Hide me from the secret
counsel of evildoers,

1. Or *One thing* 2. Or *These two things I have heard* 3. Lit *early* 4. Lit *fat*
5. Or *concern*

From the tumult of those who
do iniquity,

3 Who have sharpened their
tongue like a sword.
They aimed bitter speech *as*
their arrow,

4 To shoot from concealment at
the blameless;
Suddenly they shoot at him,
and do not fear.

5 They hold fast to themselves
an evil purpose;
They talk of laying snares
secretly;

They say, "Who can see
them?"

6 They ¹devise injustices, *saying,*
"We are ready with a
well-conceived plot";

For the inward thought and
the heart of a man are
²deep.

7 But God will shoot at them
with an arrow;
Suddenly they will be
wounded.

8 So they will make him
stumble;
Their own tongue is against
them;

All who see them will shake
the head.

9 Then all men will fear,
And they will declare the work
of God,

And will consider what He has
done.

10 The righteous man will be
glad in the LORD and will take
refuge in Him;
And all the upright in heart
will glory.

---
1. Or *search out* 2. Or *unsearchable*

PSALM 65

*God's Abundant Favor
to Earth and Man.*
For the choir director. A Psalm
of David. A Song.

1 There will be silence before
You, *and* praise in Zion, O
God,
And to You the vow will be
performed.

2 O You who hear prayer,
To You all men come.

3 Iniquities prevail against me;
As for our transgressions, You
forgive them.

4 How blessed is the one whom
You choose and bring near *to
You*
To dwell in Your courts.
We will be satisfied with the
goodness of Your house,
Your holy temple.

5 By awesome *deeds* You
answer us in righteousness, O
God of our salvation,
You who are the trust of all
the ends of the earth and of
the farthest sea;

6 Who establishes the
mountains by His strength,
Being girded with might;

7 Who stills the roaring of the
seas,
The roaring of their waves,
And the tumult of the peoples.

8 They who dwell in the ends *of
the earth* stand in awe of
Your signs;
You make the dawn and the
sunset shout for joy.

9 You visit the earth and cause
it to overflow;
You greatly enrich it;
The stream of God is full of
water;

You prepare their grain, for
thus You prepare the earth.

10 You water its furrows
abundantly,
You settle its ridges,
You soften it with showers,
You bless its growth.

11 You have crowned the year
with Your bounty,
And Your paths drip *with*
fatness.

12 The pastures of the wilderness
drip,
And the hills gird themselves
with rejoicing.

13 The meadows are clothed with
flocks
And the valleys are covered
with grain;
They shout for joy, yes, they
sing.

PSALM 66

*Praise for God's Mighty Deeds
and for His Answer to Prayer.*
For the choir director.
A Song. A Psalm.

1 Shout joyfully to God, all the
earth;

2 Sing the glory of His name;
Make His praise glorious.

3 Say to God, "How awesome
are Your works!
Because of the greatness of
Your power Your enemies
will give feigned obedience to
You.

4 "All the earth will worship
You,
And will sing praises to You;
They will sing praises to Your
name."   Selah.

5 Come and see the works of
God,

Who is awesome in *His* deeds
toward the sons of men.

6 He turned the sea into dry
land;
They passed through the river
on foot;
There let us rejoice in Him!

7 He rules by His might forever;
His eyes keep watch on the
nations;
Let not the rebellious exalt
themselves.   Selah.

8 Bless our God, O peoples,
And sound His praise abroad,

9 Who keeps us in life
And does not allow our feet to
slip.

10 For You have tried us, O God;
You have refined us as silver is
refined.

11 You brought us into the net;
You laid an oppressive burden
upon our loins.

12 You made men ride over our
heads;
We went through fire and
through water,
Yet You brought us out into *a
place of* abundance.

13 I shall come into Your house
with burnt offerings;
I shall pay You my vows,

14 Which my lips uttered
And my mouth spoke when I
was in distress.

15 I shall offer to You burnt
offerings of fat beasts,
With the smoke of rams;
I shall make *an offering of*
bulls with male goats.   Selah.

16 Come *and* hear, all who ¹fear
God,
And I will tell of what He has
done for my soul.

17 I cried to Him with my mouth,

1. Or **revere**

53

And He was extolled with my
  tongue.
18 If I [1]regard wickedness in my
  heart,
  The Lord will not hear;
19 But certainly God has heard;
  He has given heed to the voice
  of my prayer.
20 Blessed be God,
  Who has not turned away my
  prayer
  Nor His lovingkindness from
  me.

PSALM 67

*The Nations Exhorted to Praise
God.*
For the choir director;
with stringed instruments.
A Psalm. A Song.

1 God be gracious to us and
  bless us,
  And cause His face to shine
  upon us—   Selah.
2 That Your way may be known
  on the earth,
  Your salvation among all
  nations.
3 Let the peoples praise You, O
  God;
  Let all the peoples praise You.
4 Let the nations be glad and
  sing for joy;
  For You will judge the peoples
  with uprightness
  And guide the nations on the
  earth.   Selah.
5 Let the peoples praise You, O
  God;
  Let all the peoples praise You.
6 The earth has yielded its
  produce;
  God, our God, blesses us.
7 God blesses us,
  [2]That all the ends of the earth
  may fear Him.

PSALM 68

*The God of Sinai and
of the Sanctuary.*
For the choir director.
A Psalm of David. A Song.

1 Let God arise, let His enemies
  be scattered,
  And let those who hate Him
  flee before Him.
2 As smoke is driven away, *so*
  drive *them* away;
  As wax melts before the fire,
  So let the wicked perish before
  God.
3 But let the righteous be glad;
  let them exult before God;
  Yes, let them rejoice with
  gladness.
4 Sing to God, sing praises to
  His name;
  Lift up *a song* for Him who
  rides through the deserts,
  Whose name is the LORD, and
  exult before Him.
5 A father of the fatherless and
  a judge [3]for the widows,
  Is God in His holy habitation.
6 God makes a home for the
  lonely;
  He leads out the prisoners into
  prosperity,
  Only the rebellious dwell in a
  parched land.
7 O God, when You went forth
  before Your people,
  When You marched through
  the wilderness,   Selah.
8 The earth quaked;
  The heavens also dropped *rain*
  at the presence of God;
  Sinai itself *quaked* at the
  presence of God, the God of
  Israel.
9 You shed abroad a plentiful
  rain, O God;

---

1. Or *had regarded* 2. Or *And let all...earth fear Him* 3. Lit *of*

You confirmed Your
inheritance when it was
parched.
10 Your creatures settled in it;
You provided in Your
goodness for the poor, O God.

11 The Lord gives the command;
The women who proclaim the
good tidings are a great host:
12 "Kings of armies flee, they flee,
And she who remains at home
will divide the spoil!"
13 ¹When you lie down among
the ²sheepfolds,
You are like the wings of a
dove covered with silver,
And its pinions with glistening
gold.
14 When the Almighty scattered
the kings there,
It was snowing in Zalmon.

15 A mountain of God is the
mountain of Bashan;
A mountain *of many* peaks is
the mountain of Bashan.
16 Why do you look with envy, O
mountains with *many* peaks,
At the mountain which God
has desired for His abode?
Surely the Lord will dwell
there forever.
17 The chariots of God are
³myriads, thousands upon
thousands;
The Lord is among them *as at*
Sinai, in holiness.
18 You have ascended on high,
You have led captive *Your*
captives;
You have received gifts among
men,
Even *among* the rebellious
also, that the Lord God may
dwell *there*.

19 Blessed be the Lord, who daily
bears our burden,
The God *who* is our salvation.
Selah.
20 God is to us a God of
deliverances;
And to God the Lord belong
escapes from death.
21 Surely God will shatter the
head of His enemies,
The hairy crown of him who
goes on in his guilty deeds.
22 The Lord said, "I will bring
them back from Bashan.
I will bring *them* back from
the depths of the sea;
23 That your foot may shatter
them in blood,
The tongue of your dogs *may
have* its portion from *your*
enemies."

24 They have seen Your
procession, O God,
The procession of my God, my
King, into the sanctuary.
25 The singers went on, the
musicians after *them*,
In the midst of the maidens
beating tambourines.
26 Bless God in the
congregations,
Even the Lord, *you who are* of
the fountain of Israel.
27 There is Benjamin, the
youngest, ruling them,
The princes of Judah *in* their
throng,
The princes of Zebulun, the
princes of Naphtali.

28 Your God has commanded
your strength;
Show Yourself strong, O God,
who have acted on our behalf.
29 Because of Your temple at
Jerusalem
Kings will bring gifts to You.

---

1. Lit *If* 2. Or *cooking stones* or *saddle bags* 3. Lit *twice ten thousand*

30 Rebuke the beasts in the reeds,
    The herd of bulls with the
      calves of the peoples,
    Trampling under foot the
      pieces of silver;
    He has scattered the peoples
      who delight in war.
31 Envoys will come out of
      Egypt;
    Ethiopia will quickly stretch
      out her hands to God.
32 Sing to God, O kingdoms of
      the earth,
    Sing praises to the Lord,
                              Selah.
33 To Him who rides upon the
      highest heavens, which are
      from ancient times;
    Behold, He speaks forth with
      His voice, a mighty voice.
34 Ascribe strength to God;
    His majesty is over Israel
    And His strength is in the
      skies.
35 O God, *You are* awesome from
      Your sanctuary.
    The God of Israel Himself
    gives strength and power to
      the people.
    Blessed be God!

PSALM 69

*A Cry of Distress and
Imprecation on Adversaries.*
For the choir director;
according to [1]Shoshannim.
A Psalm of David.

1 Save me, O God,
    For the waters have
      threatened my life.
2 I have sunk in deep mire, and
      there is no foothold;
    I have come into deep waters,
      and a flood overflows me.

3 I am weary with my crying;
    my throat is parched;
    My eyes fail while I wait for
      my God.
4 Those who hate me without a
      cause are more than the hairs
      of my head;
    Those who would destroy me
      are powerful, being
      wrongfully my enemies;
    What I did not steal, I then
      have to restore.
5 O God, it is You who knows
      my folly,
    And my wrongs are not
      hidden from You.
6 May those who wait for You
      not be ashamed through me,
    O Lord GOD of hosts;
    May those who seek You not
      be dishonored through me, O
      God of Israel,
7 Because for Your sake I have
      borne reproach;
    Dishonor has covered my face.
8 I have become estranged from
      my brothers
    And an alien to my mother's
      sons.
9 For zeal for Your house has
      consumed me,
    And the reproaches of those
      who reproach You have
      fallen on me.
10 When I wept in my soul with
      fasting,
    It became my reproach.
11 When I made sackcloth my
      clothing,
    I became a byword to them.
12 Those who sit in the gate talk
      about me,
    And I *am* the song of the
      drunkards.
13 But as for me, my prayer is to

---
1. Or possibly *Lilies*

You, O LORD, at an
acceptable time;
O God, in the greatness of
Your lovingkindness,
Answer me with Your saving
truth.

14 Deliver me from the mire and
do not let me sink;
May I be delivered from my
foes and from the deep
waters.

15 May the flood of water not
overflow me
Nor the deep swallow me up,
Nor the pit shut its mouth on
me.

16 Answer me, O LORD, for Your
lovingkindness is good;
According to the greatness of
Your compassion, turn to me,

17 And do not hide Your face
from Your servant,
For I am in distress; answer
me quickly.

18 Oh draw near to my soul *and*
redeem it;
Ransom me because of my
enemies!

19 You know my reproach and
my shame and my dishonor;
All my adversaries are ¹before
You.

20 Reproach has broken my
heart and I am so sick.
And I looked for sympathy,
but there was none,
And for comforters, but I
found none.

21 They also gave me ²gall for my
food
And for my thirst they gave
me vinegar to drink.

22 May their table before them
become a snare;

And when they are in peace,
may it become a trap.

23 May their eyes grow dim so
that they cannot see,
And make their loins shake
continually.

24 Pour out Your indignation on
them,
And may Your burning anger
overtake them.

25 May their camp be desolate;
May none dwell in their tents.

26 For they have persecuted him
whom You Yourself have
smitten,
And they tell of the pain of
those whom You have
wounded.

27 Add iniquity to their iniquity,
And may they not come into
Your righteousness.

28 May they be blotted out of the
book of life
And may they not be recorded
with the righteous.

29 But I am afflicted and in pain;
May Your salvation, O God,
set me *securely* on high.

30 I will praise the name of God
with song
And magnify Him with
thanksgiving.

31 And it will please the LORD
better than an ox
Or a young bull with horns
and hoofs.

32 The humble have seen *it and*
are glad;
You who seek God, let your
heart revive.

33 For the LORD hears the needy
And does not despise His *who
are* prisoners.

34 Let heaven and earth praise
Him,

1. Or known *to You* 2. Or *poison*

The seas and everything that
moves in them.
35 For God will save Zion and
build the cities of Judah,
That they may dwell there and
possess it.
36 The descendants of His
servants will inherit it,
And those who love His name
will dwell in it.

PSALM 70

*Prayer for Help against
Persecutors.*

For the choir director. *A Psalm*
of David; for a memorial.

1 O God, *hasten* to deliver me;
O Lord, hasten to my help!
2 Let those be ashamed and
humiliated
Who seek my life;
Let those be turned back and
dishonored
Who delight in my hurt.
3 Let those be turned back
because of their shame
Who say, "Aha, aha!"
4 Let all who seek You rejoice
and be glad in You;
And let those who love Your
salvation say continually,
"Let God be magnified."
5 But I am afflicted and needy;
Hasten to me, O God!
You are my help and my
deliverer;
O Lord, do not delay.

PSALM 71

*Prayer of an Old Man for
Deliverance.*

1 In You, O Lord, I have taken
refuge;
Let me never be ashamed.
2 In Your righteousness deliver
me and rescue me;

Incline Your ear to me and
save me.
3 Be to me a rock of habitation
to which I may continually
come;
You have given
commandment to save me,
For You are my rock and my
fortress.
4 Rescue me, O my God, out of
the hand of the wicked,
Out of the grasp of the
wrongdoer and ruthless man,
5 For You are my hope;
O Lord God, *You are* my
confidence from my youth.
6 By You I have been sustained
from *my* birth;
You are He who took me from
my mother's womb;
My praise is continually of
You.
7 I have become a marvel to
many,
For You are my strong refuge.
8 My mouth is filled with Your
praise
And with Your glory all day
long.
9 Do not cast me off in the time
of old age;
Do not forsake me when my
strength fails.
10 For my enemies have spoken
against me;
And those who watch for my
life have consulted together,
11 Saying, "God has forsaken
him;
Pursue and seize him, for
there is no one to deliver."
12 O God, do not be far from me;
O my God, hasten to my help!
13 Let those who are adversaries
of my soul be ashamed *and*
consumed;
Let them be covered with

reproach and dishonor, who
seek to injure me.
14 But as for me, I will hope
continually,
And will praise You yet more
and more.
15 My mouth shall tell of Your
righteousness
And of Your salvation all day
long;
For I do not know the sum *of
them.*
16 I will come with the mighty
deeds of the Lord GOD;
I will make mention of Your
righteousness, Yours alone.
17 O God, You have taught me
from my youth,
And I still declare Your
wondrous deeds.
18 And even when *I am* old and
gray, O God, do not forsake
me,
Until I declare Your strength
to *this* generation,
Your power to all who are to
come.
19 For Your righteousness, O
God, *reaches* to the heavens,
You who have done great
things;
O God, who is like You?
20 You who have shown ¹me
many troubles and distresses
Will revive ¹me again,
And will bring ¹me up again
from the depths of the earth.
21 May You increase my
greatness
And turn *to* comfort me.
22 I will also praise You with a
harp,
Even Your truth, O my God;
To You I will sing praises with
the lyre,
O Holy One of Israel.

23 My lips will shout for joy
when I sing praises to You;
And my soul, which You have
redeemed.
24 My tongue also will utter Your
righteousness all day long;
For they are ashamed, for they
are humiliated who seek my
hurt.

PSALM 72

*The Reign of the Righteous King.
A Psalm* of Solomon.

1 Give the king Your
judgments, O God,
And Your righteousness to the
king's son.
2 May he judge Your people
with righteousness
And ²Your afflicted with
justice.
3 Let the mountains bring peace
to the people,
And the hills, in righteousness.
4 May he vindicate the afflicted
of the people,
Save the children of the needy
And crush the oppressor.
5 Let them fear You while the
sun *endures,*
And as long as the moon,
throughout all generations.
6 May he come down like rain
upon the mown grass,
Like showers that water the
earth.
7 In his days may the righteous
flourish,
And abundance of peace till
the moon is no more.
8 May he also rule from sea to
sea
And from the River to the
ends of the earth.

1. Another reading is *us* 2. Or *Your humble*

59

9 Let the nomads of the desert
bow before him,
And his enemies lick the dust.

10 Let the kings of Tarshish and
of the islands bring presents;
The kings of Sheba and Seba
offer gifts.

11 And let all kings bow down
before him,
All nations serve him.

12 For he will deliver the needy
when he cries for help,
The afflicted also, and him
who has no helper.

13 He will have compassion on
the poor and needy,
And the lives of the needy he
will save.

14 He will rescue their life from
oppression and violence,
And their blood will be
precious in his sight;

15 So may he live, and may the
gold of Sheba be given to him;
And let them pray for him
continually;
Let them bless him all day
long.

16 May there be abundance of
grain in the earth on top of
the mountains;
Its fruit will wave like *the
cedars of* Lebanon;
And may those from the city
flourish like vegetation of the
earth.

17 May his name endure forever;
May his name increase as long
as the sun *shines;*
And let *men* bless themselves
by him;
Let all nations call him
blessed.

18 Blessed be the Lord God, the
God of Israel,
Who alone works wonders.

19 And blessed be His glorious
name forever;
And may the whole earth be
filled with His glory.
Amen, and Amen.

20 The prayers of David the son
of Jesse are ended.

BOOK 3

PSALM 73

*The End of the Wicked
Contrasted with That of
the Righteous.*
A Psalm of Asaph.

1 Surely God is good to Israel,
To those who are pure in
heart!

2 But as for me, my feet came
close to stumbling,
My steps had almost slipped.

3 For I was envious of the
arrogant
As I saw the prosperity of the
wicked.

4 For there are no pains in their
death,
And their body is fat.

5 They are not in trouble *as
other* men,
Nor are they plagued like
mankind.

6 Therefore pride is their
necklace;
The garment of violence
covers them.

7 Their eye bulges from fatness;
The imaginations of *their*
heart run riot.

8 They mock and wickedly
speak of oppression;
They speak from on high.

9 They have set their mouth
against the heavens,
And their tongue parades
through the earth.

10 Therefore his people return to this place,
And waters of abundance are drunk by them.

11 They say, "How does God know?
And is there knowledge with the Most High?"

12 Behold, these are the wicked;
And always at ease, they have increased *in* wealth.

13 Surely in vain I have kept my heart pure
And washed my hands in innocence;

14 For I have been stricken all day long
And chastened every morning.

15 If I had said, "I will speak thus,"
Behold, I would have betrayed the generation of Your children.

16 When I pondered to understand this,
It was troublesome in my sight

17 Until I came into the sanctuary of God;
Then I perceived their end.

18 Surely You set them in slippery places;
You cast them down to destruction.

19 How they are destroyed in a moment!
They are utterly swept away by sudden terrors!

20 Like a dream when one awakes,
O Lord, when aroused, You will despise their form.

21 When my heart was embittered
And I was pierced within,

22 Then I was senseless and ignorant;
I was *like* a beast before You.

23 Nevertheless I am continually with You;
You have taken hold of my right hand.

24 With Your counsel You will guide me,
And afterward receive me to glory.

25 Whom have I in heaven *but You?*
And besides You, I desire nothing on earth.

26 My flesh and my heart may fail,
But God is the strength of my heart and my portion forever.

27 For, behold, those who are far from You will perish;
You have destroyed all those who are unfaithful to You.

28 But as for me, the nearness of God is my good;
I have made the Lord GOD my refuge,
That I may tell of all Your works.

PSALM 74

An Appeal against the Devastation of the Land by the Enemy.
A Maskil of Asaph.

1 O God, why have You rejected *us* forever?
Why does Your anger smoke against the sheep of Your pasture?

2 Remember Your congregation, which You have purchased of old,
Which You have redeemed to be the tribe of Your inheritance;
And this Mount Zion, where You have dwelt.

3 Turn Your footsteps toward the perpetual ruins;

The enemy has damaged everything within the sanctuary.

4 Your adversaries have roared in the midst of Your meeting place;
They have set up their own standards for signs.

5 It seems as if one had lifted up *His* axe in a forest of trees.

6 And now all its carved work They smash with hatchet and hammers.

7 They have burned Your sanctuary to the ground;
They have defiled the dwelling place of Your name.

8 They said in their heart, "Let us completely subdue them."
They have burned all the meeting places of God in the land.

9 We do not see our signs;
There is no longer any prophet,
Nor is there any among us who knows how long.

10 How long, O God, will the adversary revile,
And the enemy spurn Your name forever?

11 Why do You withdraw Your hand, even Your right hand?
From within Your bosom, destroy *them!*

12 Yet God is my king from of old,
Who works deeds of deliverance in the midst of the earth.

13 [1]You divided the sea by Your strength;
You broke the heads of the sea monsters in the waters.

14 You crushed the heads of Leviathan;
You gave him as food for the creatures of the wilderness.

15 You broke open springs and torrents;
You dried up ever-flowing streams.

16 Yours is the day, Yours also is the night;
You have prepared the light and the sun.

17 You have established all the boundaries of the earth;
You have made summer and winter.

18 Remember this, O Lord, that the enemy has reviled,
And a foolish people has spurned Your name.

19 Do not deliver the soul of Your turtledove to the wild beast;
Do not forget the life of Your afflicted forever.

20 Consider the covenant;
For the dark places of the land are full of the habitations of violence.

21 Let not the oppressed return dishonored;
Let the afflicted and needy praise Your name.

22 Arise, O God, *and* plead Your own cause;
Remember how the foolish man reproaches You all day long.

23 Do not forget the voice of Your adversaries,
The uproar of those who rise against You which ascends continually.

1. Or *You Yourself*

PSALM 75

*God Abases the Proud, but
Exalts the Righteous.*
For the choir director; *set to*
Al-tashheth. A Psalm of
Asaph, a Song.

1 We give thanks to You, O
   God, we give thanks,
   For Your name is near;
   Men declare Your wondrous
   works.
2 "When I select an appointed
   time,
   It is I who judge with equity.
3 "The earth and all who dwell in
   it ¹melt;
   It is I who have firmly set its
   pillars.   Selah.
4 "I said to the boastful, 'Do not
   boast,'
   And to the wicked, 'Do not lift
   up the horn;
5 Do not lift up your horn on
   high,
   Do not speak with insolent
   pride.' "
6 For not from the east, nor
   from the west,
   Nor from the desert *comes*
   exaltation;
7 But God is the Judge;
   He puts down one and exalts
   another.
8 For a cup is in the hand of the
   LORD, and the wine foams;
   It is well mixed, and He pours
   out of this;
   Surely all the wicked of the
   earth must drain *and* drink
   down its dregs.
9 But as for me, I will declare *it*
   forever;
   I will sing praises to the God
   of Jacob.

10 And all the horns of the
   wicked He will cut off,
   But the horns of the righteous
   will be lifted up.

PSALM 76

*The Victorious Power of
the God of Jacob.*
For the choir director; on stringed
instruments. A Psalm of Asaph, a
Song.

1 God is known in Judah;
   His name is great in Israel.
2 His tabernacle is in Salem;
   His dwelling place also is in
   Zion.
3 There He broke the flaming
   arrows,
   The shield and the sword and
   the weapons of war.   Selah.
4 You are resplendent,
   More majestic than the
   mountains of prey.
5 The stouthearted were
   plundered,
   They sank into sleep;
   And none of the warriors
   could use his hands.
6 At Your rebuke, O God of
   Jacob,
   Both rider and horse were cast
   into a dead sleep.
7 You, even You, are to be
   feared;
   And who may stand in Your
   presence when once You are
   angry?
8 You caused judgment to be
   heard from heaven;
   The earth feared and was still
9 When God arose to judgment,
   To save all the humble of the
   earth.   Selah.
10 For the wrath of man shall
   praise You;

---

1. Or *totter*

With a remnant of wrath You
  will gird Yourself.
11 Make vows to the LORD your
    God and fulfill *them;*
    Let all who are around Him
    bring gifts to Him who is to
    be feared.
12 He will cut off the spirit of
   princes;
   He is feared by the kings of
   the earth.

PSALM 77

*Comfort in Trouble from
Recalling God's Mighty Deeds.*
For the choir director; according
to Jeduthun. A Psalm of Asaph.

1 My voice *rises* to God, and I
  will cry aloud;
  My voice *rises* to God, and He
  will hear me.
2 In the day of my trouble I
  sought the Lord;
  In the night my hand was
  stretched out [1]without
  weariness;
  My soul refused to be
  comforted.
3 *When* I remember God, then I
  am disturbed;
  When I sigh, then my spirit
  grows faint.   Selah.
4 You have held my eyelids
  open;
  I am so troubled that I cannot
  speak.
5 I have considered the days of
  old,
  The years of long ago.
6 I will remember my song in
  the night;
  I will meditate with my heart,
  And my spirit ponders:
7 Will the Lord reject forever?

And will He never be
  favorable again?
8 Has His lovingkindness ceased
  forever?
  Has *His* promise come to an
  end forever?
9 Has God forgotten to be
  gracious,
  Or has He in anger withdrawn
  His compassion?   Selah.
10 Then I said, "It is my grief,
   That the right hand of the
   Most High has changed."
11 I shall remember the deeds of
   the LORD;
   Surely I will remember Your
   wonders of old.
12 I will meditate on all Your
   work
   And muse on Your deeds.
13 Your way, O God, is holy;
   What god is great like our
   God?
14 You are the God who works
   wonders;
   You have made known Your
   strength among the peoples.
15 You have by Your power
   redeemed Your people,
   The sons of Jacob and Joseph.
                          Selah.
16 The waters saw You, O God;
   The waters saw You, they
   were in anguish;
   The deeps also trembled.
17 The clouds poured out water;
   The skies gave forth a sound;
   Your arrows flashed here and
   there.
18 The sound of Your thunder
   was in the whirlwind;
   The lightnings lit up the
   world;
   The earth trembled and shook.
19 Your way was in the sea

1. Lit *and did not grow numb*

And Your paths in the mighty
waters,
And Your footprints may not
be known.
20 You led Your people like a
flock
By the hand of Moses and
Aaron.

PSALM 78

*God's Guidance of His People
in Spite of Their Unfaithfulness.*
A Maskil of Asaph.

1 Listen, O my people, to my
instruction;
Incline your ears to the words
of my mouth.
2 I will open my mouth in a
parable;
I will utter dark sayings of old,
3 Which we have heard and
known,
And our fathers have told us.
4 We will not conceal them from
their children,
But tell to the generation to
come the praises of the LORD,
And His strength and His
wondrous works that He has
done.
5 For He established a
testimony in Jacob
And appointed a law in Israel,
Which He commanded our
fathers
That they should teach them
to their children,
6 That the generation to come
might know, *even* the
children *yet* to be born,
That they may arise and tell
them to their children,
7 That they should put their
confidence in God

And not forget the works of
God,
But keep His commandments,
8 And not be like their fathers,
A stubborn and rebellious
generation,
A generation that did not
¹prepare its heart
And whose spirit was not
faithful to God.
9 The sons of Ephraim were
archers equipped with bows,
Yet they turned back in the
day of battle.
10 They did not keep the
covenant of God
And refused to walk in His
law;
11 They forgot His deeds
And His miracles that He had
shown them.
12 He wrought wonders before
their fathers
In the land of Egypt, in the
field of Zoan.
13 He divided the sea and caused
them to pass through,
And He made the waters
stand up like a heap.
14 Then He led them with the
cloud by day
And all the night with a light
of fire.
15 He split the rocks in the
wilderness
And gave *them* abundant
drink like the ocean depths.
16 He brought forth streams also
from the rock
And caused waters to run
down like rivers.
17 Yet they still continued to sin
against Him,
To rebel against the Most
High in the desert.

1. Or *put right*

65

18 And in their heart they put God to the test
   By asking food according to their desire.
19 Then they spoke against God;
   They said, "Can God prepare a table in the wilderness?
20 "Behold, He struck the rock so that waters gushed out,
   And streams were overflowing;
   Can He give bread also?
   Will He provide meat for His people?"
21 Therefore the LORD heard and was full of wrath;
   And a fire was kindled against Jacob
   And anger also mounted against Israel.
22 Because they did not believe in God
   And did not trust in His salvation.
23 Yet He commanded the clouds above
   And opened the doors of heaven;
24 He rained down manna upon them to eat
   And gave them food from heaven.
25 Man did eat the bread of angels;
   He sent them food in abundance.
26 He caused the east wind to blow in the heavens
   And by His power He directed the south wind.
27 When He rained meat upon them like the dust,
   Even winged fowl like the sand of the seas,
28 Then He let *them* fall in the midst of their camp,
   Round about their dwellings.
29 So they ate and were well filled,
   And their desire He gave to them.
30 Before they had satisfied their desire,
   While their food was in their mouths,
31 The anger of God rose against them
   And killed some of their stoutest ones,
   And subdued the choice men of Israel.
32 In spite of all this they still sinned
   And did not believe in His wonderful works.
33 So He brought their days to an end in futility
   And their years in sudden terror.
34 When He killed them, then they sought Him,
   And returned and searched diligently for God;
35 And they remembered that God was their rock,
   And the Most High God their Redeemer.
36 But they deceived Him with their mouth
   And lied to Him with their tongue.
37 For their heart was not steadfast toward Him,
   Nor were they faithful in His covenant.
38 But He, being compassionate, forgave *their* iniquity and did not destroy *them*;
   And often He restrained His anger
   And did not arouse all His wrath.
39 Thus He remembered that they were but flesh,

66

A wind that passes and does not return.

40 How often they rebelled against Him in the wilderness And grieved Him in the desert!

41 Again and again they [1]tempted God, And pained the Holy One of Israel.

42 They did not remember His power, The day when He redeemed them from the adversary,

43 When He performed His signs in Egypt And His marvels in the field of Zoan,

44 And turned their rivers to blood, And their streams, they could not drink.

45 He sent among them swarms of flies which devoured them, And frogs which destroyed them.

46 He gave also their crops to the grasshopper And the product of their labor to the locust.

47 He destroyed their vines with hailstones And their sycamore trees with frost.

48 He gave over their cattle also to the hailstones And their herds to bolts of lightning.

49 He sent upon them His burning anger, Fury and indignation and trouble, A band of destroying angels.

50 He leveled a path for His anger;

He did not spare their soul from death, But gave over their life to the plague;

51 And smote all the firstborn in Egypt, The first *issue* of their virility in the tents of Ham.

52 But He led forth His own people like sheep And guided them in the wilderness like a flock;

53 He led them safely, so that they did not fear; But the sea engulfed their enemies.

54 So He brought them to His holy land, To this hill country which His right hand had gained.

55 He also drove out the nations before them And apportioned them for an inheritance by measurement, And made the tribes of Israel dwell in their tents.

56 Yet they [2]tempted and rebelled against the Most High God And did not keep His testimonies,

57 But turned back and acted treacherously like their fathers; They turned aside like a treacherous bow.

58 For they provoked Him with their high places And aroused His jealousy with their graven images.

59 When God heard, He was filled with wrath And greatly abhorred Israel;

60 So that He abandoned the dwelling place at Shiloh,

---

1. Or *put God to the test* 2. Or *put to the test*

The tent which He had
pitched among men,

61 And gave up His strength to
captivity
And His glory into the hand of
the adversary.

62 He also delivered His people
to the sword,
And was filled with wrath at
His inheritance.

63 Fire devoured His young men,
And His virgins had no
wedding songs.

64 His priests fell by the sword,
And His widows could not
weep.

65 Then the Lord awoke as *if
from* sleep,
Like a warrior overcome by
wine.

66 He drove His adversaries
backward;
He put on them an everlasting
reproach.

67 He also rejected the tent of
Joseph,
And did not choose the tribe
of Ephraim,

68 But chose the tribe of Judah,
Mount Zion which He loved.

69 And He built His sanctuary
like the heights,
Like the earth which He has
founded forever.

70 He also chose David His
servant
And took him from the
sheepfolds;

71 From the care of the ewes with
suckling lambs He brought
him
To shepherd Jacob His people,
And Israel His inheritance.

72 So he shepherded them
according to the integrity of
his heart,

And guided them with his
skillful hands.

PSALM 79

*A Lament over the Destruction
of Jerusalem, and Prayer
for Help.*
A Psalm of Asaph.

1 O God, the nations have
invaded Your inheritance;
They have defiled Your holy
temple;
They have laid Jerusalem in
ruins.

2 They have given the dead
bodies of Your servants for
food to the birds of the
heavens,
The flesh of Your godly ones
to the beasts of the earth.

3 They have poured out their
blood like water round about
Jerusalem;
And there was no one to bury
them.

4 We have become a reproach to
our neighbors,
A scoffing and derision to
those around us.

5 How long, O LORD? Will You
be angry forever?
Will Your jealousy burn like
fire?

6 Pour out Your wrath upon the
nations which do not know
You,
And upon the kingdoms
which do not call upon Your
name.

7 For they have devoured Jacob
And laid waste his habitation.

8 Do not remember the
iniquities of *our* forefathers
against us;
Let Your compassion come
quickly to meet us,
For we are brought very low.

9 Help us, O God of our
salvation, for the glory of
Your name;
And deliver us and forgive our
sins for Your name's sake.
10 Why should the nations say,
"Where is their God?"
Let there be known among the
nations in our sight,
Vengeance for the blood of
Your servants which has been
shed.
11 Let the groaning of the
prisoner come before You;
According to the greatness of
Your power preserve those
who are doomed to die.
12 And return to our neighbors
sevenfold into their bosom
The reproach with which they
have reproached You, O
Lord.
13 So we Your people and the
sheep of Your pasture
Will give thanks to You
forever;
To all generations we will tell
of Your praise.

PSALM 80

*God Implored to Rescue His
People from Their Calamities.*
For the choir director; *set to*
El Shoshannim; Eduth.
A Psalm of Asaph.

1 Oh, give ear, Shepherd of
Israel,
You who lead Joseph like a
flock;
You who are enthroned *above*
the cherubim, shine forth!
2 Before Ephraim and
Benjamin and Manasseh, stir
up Your power
And come to save us!
3 O God, restore us
And cause Your face to shine
upon us, and we will be
saved.

4 O LORD God *of* hosts,
How long will You be angry
with the prayer of Your
people?
5 You have fed them with the
bread of tears,
And You have made them to
drink tears in large measure.
6 You make us [1]an object of
contention to our neighbors,
And our enemies laugh among
themselves.
7 O God *of* hosts, restore us
And cause Your face to shine
upon us, [2]and we will be
saved.

8 You removed a vine from
Egypt;
You drove out the nations and
planted it.
9 You cleared *the ground* before
it,
And it took deep root and
filled the land.
10 The mountains were covered
with its shadow,
And the cedars of God with its
boughs.
11 It was sending out its branches
to the sea
And its shoots to the River.
12 Why have You broken down
its hedges,
So that all who pass *that* way
pick its *fruit*?
13 A boar from the forest eats it
away
And whatever moves in the
field feeds on it.

14 O God *of* hosts, turn again
now, we beseech You;

1. Lit *a strife to* 2. Or *that we may*

69

Look down from heaven and
see, and take care of this vine,
15 Even the shoot which Your
right hand has planted,
And on the son whom You
have strengthened for
Yourself.
16 It is burned with fire, it is cut
down;
They perish at the rebuke of
Your countenance.
17 Let Your hand be upon the
man of Your right hand,
Upon the son of man whom
You made strong for
Yourself.
18 Then we shall not turn back
from You;
Revive us, and we will call
upon Your name.
19 O LORD God of hosts, restore
us;
Cause Your face to shine *upon
us*, and we will be saved.

PSALM 81

*God's Goodness and
Israel's Waywardness.*
For the choir director; on the
Gittith. *A Psalm* of Asaph.

1 Sing for joy to God our
strength;
Shout joyfully to the God of
Jacob.
2 Raise a song, strike the
timbrel,
The sweet sounding lyre with
the harp.
3 Blow the trumpet at the new
moon,
At the full moon, on our feast
day.
4 For it is a statute for Israel,
An ordinance of the God of
Jacob.
5 He established it for a
testimony in Joseph

When he went throughout the
land of Egypt.
I heard a language that I did
not know:
6 "I relieved his shoulder of the
burden,
His hands were freed from the
basket.
7 "You called in trouble and I
rescued you;
I answered you in the hiding
place of thunder;
I proved you at the waters of
Meribah.   Selah.
8 "Hear, O My people, and I will
admonish you;
O Israel, if you would listen to
Me!
9 "Let there be no strange god
among you;
Nor shall you worship any
foreign god.
10 "I, the LORD, am your God,
Who brought you up from the
land of Egypt;
Open your mouth wide and I
will fill it.
11 "But My people did not listen
to My voice,
And Israel did not obey Me.
12 "So I gave them over to the
stubbornness of their heart,
To walk in their own devices.
13 "Oh that My people would
listen to Me,
That Israel would walk in My
ways!
14 "I would quickly subdue their
enemies
And turn My hand against
their adversaries.
15 "Those who hate the LORD
would pretend obedience to
Him,
And their time *of punishment*
would be forever.

16 "But I would feed you with the
   finest of the wheat,
   And with honey from the rock
   I would satisfy you."

PSALM 82

Unjust Judgments Rebuked.
A Psalm of Asaph.

1 God takes His stand in His
   own congregation;
   He judges in the midst of the
   rulers.
2 How long will you judge
   unjustly
   And show partiality to the
   wicked?   Selah.
3 Vindicate the weak and
   fatherless;
   Do justice to the afflicted and
   destitute.
4 Rescue the weak and needy;
   Deliver *them* out of the hand
   of the wicked.
5 They do not know nor do they
   understand;
   They walk about in darkness;
   All the foundations of the
   earth are shaken.
6 I said, "You are gods,
   And all of you are sons of the
   Most High.
7 "Nevertheless you will die like
   men
   And fall like *any* one of the
   princes."
8 Arise, O God, judge the earth!
   For it is You who possesses all
   the nations.

PSALM 83

*God Implored to Confound
His Enemies.*
A Song, a Psalm of Asaph.

1 O God, do not remain quiet;
   Do not be silent and, O God,
   do not be still.

2 For behold, Your enemies
   make an uproar,
   And those who hate You have
   exalted themselves.
3 They make shrewd plans
   against Your people,
   And conspire together against
   Your treasured ones.
4 They have said, "Come, and
   let us wipe them out as a
   nation,
   That the name of Israel be
   remembered no more."
5 For they have conspired
   together with one mind;
   Against You they make a
   covenant:
6 The tents of Edom and the
   Ishmaelites,
   Moab and the Hagrites;
7 Gebal and Ammon and
   Amalek,
   Philistia with the inhabitants
   of Tyre;
8 Assyria also has joined with
   them;
   They have become a help to
   the children of Lot.   Selah.
9 Deal with them as with
   Midian,
   As with Sisera *and* Jabin at
   the torrent of Kishon,
10 Who were destroyed at
   En-dor,
   Who became as dung for the
   ground.
11 Make their nobles like Oreb
   and Zeeb
   And all their princes like
   Zebah and Zalmunna,
12 Who said, "Let us possess for
   ourselves
   The pastures of God."
13 O my God, make them like the
   whirling dust,
   Like chaff before the wind.
14 Like fire that burns the forest

71

And like a flame that sets the
mountains on fire,

15 So pursue them with Your
tempest
And terrify them with Your
storm.

16 Fill their faces with dishonor,
That they may seek Your
name, O Lord.

17 Let them be ashamed and
dismayed forever,
And let them be humiliated
and perish,

18 That they may know that You
alone, whose name is the
Lord,
Are the Most High over all the
earth.

PSALM 84

Longing for the Temple Worship.
For the choir director; on the
Gittith. A Psalm of the
sons of Korah.

1 How lovely are Your dwelling
places,
O Lord of hosts!

2 My soul longed and even
yearned for the courts of the
Lord;
My heart and my flesh sing for
joy to the living God.

3 The bird also has found a
house,
And the swallow a nest for
herself, where she may lay
her young,
Even Your altars, O Lord of
hosts,
My King and my God.

4 How blessed are those who
dwell in Your house!
They are ever praising You.
Selah.

5 How blessed is the man whose
strength is in You,
In whose heart are the
highways *to Zion!*

6 Passing through the valley of
[1]Baca they make it a spring;
The early rain also covers it
with blessings.

7 They go from strength to
strength,
Every one of them appears
before God in Zion.

8 O Lord God of hosts, hear my
prayer;
Give ear, O God of Jacob!
Selah.

9 Behold our shield, O God,
And look upon the face of
Your anointed.

10 For a day in Your courts is
better than a thousand
outside.
I would rather stand at the
threshold of the house of my
God
Than dwell in the tents of
wickedness.

11 For the Lord God is a sun and
shield;
The Lord gives grace and
glory;
No good thing does He
withhold from those who
walk uprightly.

12 O Lord of hosts,
How blessed is the man who
trusts in You!

PSALM 85

*Prayer for God's Mercy
upon the Nation.*
For the choir director. A Psalm of
the sons of Korah.

1 O Lord, You showed favor to
Your land;

---

1. Probably, *Weeping;* or *Balsam trees*

72

You ¹restored the captivity of
Jacob.

2 You forgave the iniquity of
Your people;
You covered all their sin.
Selah.

3 You withdrew all Your fury;
You turned away from Your
burning anger.

4 Restore us, O God of our
salvation,
And cause Your indignation
toward us to cease.

5 Will You be angry with us
forever?
Will You prolong Your anger
to all generations?

6 Will You not Yourself revive
us again,
That Your people may rejoice
in You?

7 Show us Your lovingkindness,
O LORD,
And grant us Your salvation.

8 I will hear what God the LORD
will say;
For He will speak peace to His
people, to His godly ones;
But let them not turn back to
folly.

9 Surely His salvation is near to
those who ²fear Him,
That glory may dwell in our
land.

10 Lovingkindness and truth
have met together;
Righteousness and peace have
kissed each other.

11 Truth springs from the earth,
And righteousness looks down
from heaven.

12 Indeed, the LORD will give
what is good,
And our land will yield its
produce.

13 Righteousness will go before
Him
And will make His footsteps
into a way.

PSALM 86

*A Psalm of Supplication
and Trust.*
A Prayer of David.

1 Incline Your ear, O LORD, *and*
answer me;
For I am afflicted and needy.

2 Preserve my soul, for I am a
godly man;
O You my God, save Your
servant who trusts in You.

3 Be gracious to me, O Lord,
For to You I cry all day long.

4 Make glad the soul of Your
servant,
For to You, O Lord, I lift up
my soul.

5 For You, Lord, are good, and
ready to forgive,
And abundant in
lovingkindness to all who call
upon You.

6 Give ear, O LORD, to my
prayer;
And give heed to the voice of
my supplications!

7 In the day of my trouble I
shall call upon You,
For You will answer me.

8 There is no one like You
among the gods, O Lord,
Nor are there any works like
Yours.

9 All nations whom You have
made shall come and worship
before You, O Lord,
And they shall glorify Your
name.

10 For You are great and do
wondrous deeds;
You alone are God.

---

1. Or *restore the fortunes* 2. Or *reverence*

11 Teach me Your way, O Lord;
I will walk in Your truth;
Unite my heart to fear Your
name.

12 I will give thanks to You, O
Lord my God, with all my
heart,
And will glorify Your name
forever.

13 For Your lovingkindness
toward me is great,
And You have delivered my
soul from the depths of Sheol.

14 O God, arrogant men have
risen up against me,
And a band of violent men
have sought my life,
And they have not set You
before them.

15 But You, O Lord, are a God
merciful and gracious,
Slow to anger and abundant in
lovingkindness and truth.

16 Turn to me, and be gracious to
me;
Oh grant Your strength to
Your servant,
And save the son of Your
handmaid.

17 Show me a sign for good,
That those who hate me may
see *it* and be ashamed,
Because You, O Lord, have
helped me and comforted me.

PSALM 87

*The Privileges of
Citizenship in Zion.*
A Psalm of the sons of Korah.
A Song.

1 His foundation is in the holy
mountains.

2 The Lord loves the gates of
Zion

More than all the *other*
dwelling places of Jacob.

3 Glorious things are spoken of
you,
O city of God.   Selah.

4 "I shall mention ¹Rahab and
Babylon among those who
know Me;
Behold, Philistia and Tyre
with Ethiopia:
'This one was born there.' "

5 But of Zion it shall be said,
"This one and that one were
born in her";
And the Most High Himself
will establish her.

6 The Lord will count when He
registers the peoples,
"This one was born there."
                        Selah.

7 Then those who sing as well as
those who play the flutes
shall say,
"All my springs *of joy* are in
you."

PSALM 88

*A Petition to Be Saved
from Death.*
A Song. A Psalm of the sons of
Korah. For the choir director;
according to Mahalath Leannoth.
A Maskil of Heman the Ezrahite.

1 O Lord, the God of my
salvation,
I have cried out by day and in
the night before You.

2 Let my prayer come before
You;
Incline Your ear to my cry!

3 For my soul has had enough
troubles,
And my life has drawn near to
Sheol.

4 I am reckoned among those
who go down to the pit;

---

1. I.e. Egypt

74

I have become like a man
without strength,

5 Forsaken among the dead,
Like the slain who lie in the
grave,
Whom You remember no
more,
And they are cut off from
Your hand.

6 You have put me in the lowest
pit,
In dark places, in the depths.

7 Your wrath has rested upon
me,
And You have afflicted me
with all Your waves. Selah.

8 You have removed my
acquaintances far from me;
You have made me an ¹object
of loathing to them;
I am shut up and cannot go
out.

9 My eye has wasted away
because of affliction;
I have called upon You every
day, O LORD;
I have spread out my hands to
You.

10 Will You perform wonders for
the dead?
Will the departed spirits rise
and praise You? Selah.

11 Will Your lovingkindness be
declared in the grave,
Your faithfulness in Abaddon?

12 Will Your wonders be made
known in the darkness?
And Your righteousness in the
land of forgetfulness?

13 But I, O LORD, have cried out
to You for help,
And in the morning my prayer
comes before You.

14 O LORD, why do You reject my
soul?

Why do You hide Your face
from me?

15 I was afflicted and about to
die from my youth on;
I suffer Your terrors; I am
overcome.

16 Your burning anger has
passed over me;
Your terrors have destroyed
me.

17 They have surrounded me like
water all day long;
They have encompassed me
altogether.

18 You have removed lover and
friend far from me;
My acquaintances are *in*
darkness.

PSALM 89

*The LORD's Covenant with David,
and Israel's Afflictions.*
A Maskil of Ethan the Ezrahite.

1 I will sing of the
lovingkindness of the LORD
forever;
To all generations I will make
known Your faithfulness with
my mouth.

2 For I have said,
"Lovingkindness will be built
up forever;
In the heavens You will
establish Your faithfulness."

3 "I have made a covenant with
My chosen;
I have sworn to David My
servant,

4 I will establish your seed
forever
And build up your throne to
all generations." Selah.

5 The heavens will praise Your
wonders, O LORD;

---

1. Lit *abomination to them*

Your faithfulness also in the
assembly of the holy ones.

6 For who in the skies is
comparable to the LORD?
Who among the sons of the
mighty is like the LORD,

7 A God greatly feared in the
council of the holy ones,
And awesome above all those
who are around Him?

8 O LORD God of hosts, who is
like You, O mighty LORD?
Your faithfulness also
surrounds You.

9 You rule the swelling of the
sea;
When its waves rise, You still
them.

10 You Yourself crushed Rahab
like one who is slain;
You scattered Your enemies
with Your mighty arm.

11 The heavens are Yours, the
earth also is Yours;
The world and ¹all it contains,
You have founded them.

12 The north and the south, You
have created them;
Tabor and Hermon shout for
joy at Your name.

13 You have a strong arm;
Your hand is mighty, Your
right hand is exalted.

14 Righteousness and justice are
the foundation of Your
throne;
Lovingkindness and truth go
before You.

15 How blessed are the people
who know the ²joyful sound!
O LORD, they walk in the light
of Your countenance.

16 In Your name they rejoice all
the day,

And by Your righteousness
they are exalted.

17 For You are the glory of their
strength,
And by Your favor our horn is
exalted.

18 For our shield belongs to the
LORD,
³And our king to the Holy One
of Israel.

19 Once You spoke in vision to
Your godly ones,
And said, "I have given help
to one who is mighty;
I have exalted one chosen
from the people.

20 "I have found David My
servant;
With My holy oil I have
anointed him,

21 With whom My hand will be
established;
My arm also will strengthen
him.

22 "The enemy will not ⁴deceive
him,
Nor the son of wickedness
afflict him.

23 "But I shall crush his
adversaries before him,
And strike those who hate
him.

24 "My faithfulness and My
lovingkindness will be with
him,
And in My name his horn will
be exalted.

25 "I shall also set his hand on the
sea
And his right hand on the
rivers.

26 "He will cry to Me, 'You are my
Father,
My God, and the rock of my
salvation.'

1. Lit *its fullness* 2. Or *blast of the trumpet, shout of joy* 3. Or *Even to the Holy One of Israel our King* 4. Or *exact usury from him*

27"I also shall make him *My* firstborn,
The highest of the kings of the earth.

28"My lovingkindness I will keep for him forever,
And My covenant shall be confirmed to him.

29"So I will establish his descendants forever
And his throne as the days of heaven.

30"If his sons forsake My law
And do not walk in My judgments,

31 If they ¹violate My statutes
And do not keep My commandments,

32 Then I will punish their transgression with the rod
And their iniquity with stripes.

33"But I will not break off My lovingkindness from him,
Nor deal falsely in My faithfulness.

34"My covenant I will not violate,
Nor will I alter the utterance of My lips.

35"²Once I have sworn by My holiness;
I will not lie to David.

36"His descendants shall endure forever
And his throne as the sun before Me.

37"It shall be established forever like the moon,
And the witness in the sky is faithful."   Selah.

38 But You have cast off and rejected,
You have been full of wrath against Your anointed.

39 You have spurned the covenant of Your servant;
You have profaned his crown in the dust.

40 You have broken down all his walls;
You have brought his strongholds to ruin.

41 All who pass along the way plunder him;
He has become a reproach to his neighbors.

42 You have exalted the right hand of his adversaries;
You have made all his enemies rejoice.

43 You also turn back the edge of his sword
And have not made him stand in battle.

44 You have made his splendor to cease
And cast his throne to the ground.

45 You have shortened the days of his youth;
You have covered him with shame.   Selah.

46 How long, O LORD?
Will You hide Yourself forever?
Will Your wrath burn like fire?

47 Remember what my span of life is;
For what vanity You have created all the sons of men!

48 What man can live and not see death?
Can he deliver his soul from the power of Sheol?   Selah.

49 Where are Your former lovingkindnesses, O Lord,
Which You swore to David in Your faithfulness?

50 Remember, O Lord, the reproach of Your servants;
How I bear in my bosom *the*

1. Lit *profane* 2. Or *One thing*

reproach of all the many peoples,

51 With which Your enemies have reproached, O LORD, With which they have reproached the footsteps of Your anointed.

52 Blessed be the LORD forever! Amen and Amen.

BOOK 4
PSALM 90

God's Eternity and Man's Transitoriness.
A Prayer of Moses, the man of God.

1 Lord, You have been our ¹dwelling place in all generations.

2 Before the mountains were born Or You gave birth to the earth and the world,

Even from everlasting to everlasting, You are God.

3 You turn man back into dust And say, "Return, O children of men."

4 For a thousand years in Your sight Are like yesterday when it passes by,

Or *as* a watch in the night.

5 You have swept them away like a flood, they fall asleep; In the morning they are like grass which sprouts anew.

6 In the morning it flourishes and sprouts anew; Toward evening it fades and withers away.

7 For we have been consumed by Your anger

And by Your wrath we have been dismayed.

8 You have placed our iniquities before You, Our secret *sins* in the light of Your presence.

9 For all our days have declined in Your fury; We have finished our years like a sigh.

10 As for the days of our life, they contain seventy years, Or if due to strength, eighty years, Yet their pride is *but* labor and sorrow; For soon it is gone and we fly away.

11 Who understands the power of Your anger And Your fury, according to the fear that is due You?

12 So teach us to number our days, That we may present to You a heart of wisdom.

13 Do return, O LORD; how long *will it be?* And be sorry for Your servants.

14 O satisfy us in the morning with Your lovingkindness, That we may sing for joy and be glad all our days.

15 Make us glad according to the days You have afflicted us, *And* the years we have seen ²evil.

16 Let Your work appear to Your servants And Your majesty to their children.

17 Let the favor of the Lord our God be upon us;

---

1. Or *hiding place;* some ancient mss read *place of refuge* 2. Or *trouble*

And ¹confirm for us the work
of our hands;
Yes, ¹confirm the work of our
hands.

PSALM 91

*Security of the One Who
Trusts in the LORD.*

1 He who dwells in the shelter of
the Most High
Will abide in the shadow of
the Almighty.
2 I will say to the LORD, "My
refuge and my fortress,
My God, in whom I trust!"
3 For it is He who delivers you
from the snare of the trapper
And from the deadly
pestilence.
4 He will cover you with His
pinions,
And under His wings you may
seek refuge;
His faithfulness is a shield and
bulwark.
5 You will not be afraid of the
terror by night,
Or of the arrow that flies by
day;
6 Of the pestilence that stalks in
darkness,
Or of the destruction that lays
waste at noon.
7 A thousand may fall at your
side
And ten thousand at your
right hand,
But it shall not approach you.
8 You will only look on with
your eyes
And see the recompense of the
wicked.
9 For you have made the LORD,
my refuge,

Even the Most High, your
dwelling place.
10 No evil will befall you,
Nor will any plague come near
your tent.
11 For He will give His angels
charge concerning you,
To guard you in all your ways.
12 They will bear you up in their
hands,
That you do not strike your
foot against a stone.
13 You will tread upon the lion
and cobra,
The young lion and the
serpent you will trample
down.
14 "Because he has loved Me,
therefore I will deliver him;
I will set him *securely* on high,
because he has known My
name.
15 "He will call upon Me, and I
will answer him;
I will be with him in trouble;
I will rescue him and honor
him.
16 "With a long life I will satisfy
him
And let him see My
salvation."

PSALM 92

Praise for the LORD's Goodness.
A Psalm, a Song for the
Sabbath day.

1 It is good to give thanks to the
LORD
And to sing praises to Your
name, O Most High;
2 To declare Your
lovingkindness in the
morning
And Your faithfulness by
night,

1. Or *give permanence to*

79

3 With the ten-stringed lute and
   with the harp,
   With resounding music upon
   the lyre.
4 For You, O LORD, have made
   me glad by what You have
   done,
   I will sing for joy at the works
   of Your hands.
5 How great are Your works, O
   LORD!
   Your thoughts are very deep.
6 A senseless man has no
   knowledge,
   Nor does a stupid man
   understand this:
7 That when the wicked
   sprouted up like grass
   And all who did iniquity
   flourished,
   It *was only* that they might be
   destroyed forevermore.
8 But You, O LORD, are on high
   forever.
9 For, behold, Your enemies, O
   LORD,
   For, behold, Your enemies will
   perish;
   All who do iniquity will be
   scattered.
10 But You have exalted my horn
   like *that of* the wild ox;
   I have been anointed with
   fresh oil.
11 And my eye has looked
   exultantly upon my foes,
   My ears hear of the evildoers
   who rise up against me.
12 The righteous man will
   flourish like the palm tree,
   He will grow like a cedar in
   Lebanon.
13 Planted in the house of the
   LORD,
   They will flourish in the courts
   of our God.

14 They will still yield fruit in old
   age;
   They shall be ¹full of sap and
   very green,
15 To declare that the LORD is
   upright;
   He is my rock, and there is no
   unrighteousness in Him.

PSALM 93

The Majesty of the LORD.

1 The LORD reigns, He is clothed
   with majesty;
   The LORD has clothed and
   girded Himself with strength;
   Indeed, the world is firmly
   established, it will not be
   moved.
2 Your throne is established
   from of old;
   You are from everlasting.
3 The floods have lifted up, O
   LORD,
   The floods have lifted up their
   voice,
   The floods lift up their
   pounding waves.
4 More than the sounds of many
   waters,
   Than the mighty breakers of
   the sea,
   The LORD on high is mighty.
5 Your testimonies are fully
   confirmed;
   Holiness befits Your house,
   O LORD, forevermore.

PSALM 94

*The LORD Implored to
Avenge His People.*

1 O LORD, God of vengeance,
   God of vengeance, shine forth!
2 Rise up, O Judge of the earth,
   Render recompense to the
   proud.

---

1. Lit *fat and*

3 How long shall the wicked, O
LORD,
How long shall the wicked
exult?
4 They pour forth *words,* they
speak arrogantly;
All who do wickedness vaunt
themselves.
5 They crush Your people, O
LORD,
And afflict Your heritage.
6 They slay the widow and the
stranger
And murder the orphans.
7 They have said, "The LORD
does not see,
Nor does the God of Jacob
pay heed."
8 Pay heed, you senseless among
the people;
And when will you
understand, stupid ones?
9 He who planted the ear, does
He not hear?
He who formed the eye, does
He not see?
10 He who chastens the nations,
will He not rebuke,
Even He who teaches man
knowledge?
11 The LORD knows the thoughts
of man,
That they are a *mere* breath.
12 Blessed is the man whom You
chasten, O LORD,
And whom You teach out of
Your law;
13 That You may grant him relief
from the days of adversity,
Until a pit is dug for the
wicked.
14 For the LORD will not abandon
His people,
Nor will He forsake His
inheritance.
15 For judgment will again be
righteous,

And all the upright in heart
will follow it.
16 Who will stand up for me
against evildoers?
Who will take his stand for me
against those who do
wickedness?
17 If the LORD had not been my
help,
My soul would soon have
dwelt in *the abode of* silence.
18 If I should say, "My foot has
slipped,"
Your lovingkindness, O LORD,
will hold me up.
19 When my anxious thoughts
multiply within me,
Your consolations delight my
soul.
20 Can a throne of destruction be
allied with You,
One which devises mischief by
decree?
21 They band themselves
together against the life of the
righteous
And condemn the innocent to
death.
22 But the LORD has been my
stronghold,
And my God the rock of my
refuge.
23 He has brought back their
wickedness upon them
And will destroy them in their
evil;
The LORD our God will
destroy them.

PSALM 95

*Praise to the LORD, and
Warning against Unbelief.*

1 O come, let us sing for joy to
the LORD,
Let us shout joyfully to the
rock of our salvation.

81

2 Let us come before His
presence with thanksgiving,
Let us shout joyfully to Him
with psalms.
3 For the LORD is a great God
And a great King above all
gods,
4 In whose hand are the depths
of the earth,
The peaks of the mountains
are His also.
5 The sea is His, for it was He
who made it,
And His hands formed the dry
land.
6 Come, let us worship and bow
down,
Let us kneel before the LORD
our Maker.
7 For He is our God,
And we are the people of His
pasture and the sheep of His
hand.

Today, if you would hear His
voice,
8 Do not harden your hearts, as
at [1]Meribah,
As in the day of [2]Massah in
the wilderness,
9 "When your fathers tested Me,
They tried Me, though they
had seen My work.
10 "For forty years I loathed *that*
generation,
And said they are a people
who err in their heart,
And they do not know My
ways.
11 "Therefore I swore in My
anger,
Truly they shall not enter into
My rest."

PSALM 96

*A Call to Worship the LORD
the Righteous Judge.*

1 Sing to the LORD a new song;
Sing to the LORD, all the earth.
2 Sing to the LORD, bless His
name;
Proclaim good tidings of His
salvation from day to day.
3 Tell of His glory among the
nations,
His wonderful deeds among
all the peoples.
4 For great is the LORD and
greatly to be praised;
He is to be feared above all
gods.
5 For all the gods of the peoples
are idols,
But the LORD made the
heavens.
6 Splendor and majesty are
before Him,
Strength and beauty are in His
sanctuary.
7 [3]Ascribe to the LORD, O
families of the peoples,
[3]Ascribe to the LORD glory and
strength.
8 [4]Ascribe to the LORD the glory
of His name;
Bring an offering and come
into His courts.
9 Worship the LORD in [5]holy
attire;
Tremble before Him, all the
earth.
10 Say among the nations, "The
LORD reigns;
Indeed, the world is firmly
established, it will not be
moved;
He will judge the peoples with
[6]equity."

1. Or *place of strife* 2. Or *temptation* 3. Lit *Give* 4. Lit *Give* 5. Or *the splendor of
holiness* 6. Or *uprightness*

82

11 Let the heavens be glad, and
let the earth rejoice;
Let the sea roar, and all it
contains;
12 Let the field exult, and all that
is in it.
Then all the trees of the forest
will sing for joy
13 Before the LORD, for He is
coming,
For He is coming to judge the
earth.
He will judge the world in
righteousness
And the peoples in His
faithfulness.

PSALM 97

The LORD'S Power and Dominion.

1 The LORD reigns, let the earth
rejoice;
Let the many ¹islands be glad.
2 Clouds and thick darkness
surround Him;
Righteousness and justice are
the foundation of His throne.
3 Fire goes before Him
And burns up His adversaries
round about.
4 His lightnings lit up the world;
The earth saw and trembled.
5 The mountains melted like
wax at the presence of the
LORD,
At the presence of the Lord of
the whole earth.
6 The heavens declare His
righteousness,
And all the peoples have seen
His glory.
7 Let all those be ashamed who
serve graven images,
Who boast themselves of idols;
Worship Him, all you gods.
8 Zion heard *this* and was glad,

And the daughters of Judah
have rejoiced
Because of Your judgments, O
LORD.
9 For You are the LORD Most
High over all the earth;
You are exalted far above all
gods.
10 Hate evil, you who love the
LORD,
Who preserves the souls of His
godly ones;
He delivers them from the
hand of the wicked.
11 Light is sown *like seed* for the
righteous
And gladness for the upright
in heart.
12 Be glad in the LORD, you
righteous ones,
And give thanks to His holy
name.

PSALM 98

*A Call to Praise the LORD
for His Righteousness.*
A Psalm.

1 O sing to the LORD a new song,
For He has done wonderful
things,
His right hand and His holy
arm have ²gained the victory
for Him.
2 The LORD has made known
His salvation;
He has revealed His
righteousness in the sight of
the nations.
3 He has remembered His
lovingkindness and His
faithfulness to the house of
Israel;
All the ends of the earth have
seen the salvation of our God.

---

1. Or *coastlands* 2. Or *accomplished salvation*

83

4 Shout joyfully to the L ord, all
the earth;
Break forth and sing for joy
and sing praises.
5 Sing praises to the L ord with
the lyre,
With the lyre and the sound of
melody.
6 With trumpets and the sound
of the horn
Shout joyfully before the King,
the L ord.
7 Let the sea roar and all it
contains,
The world and those who
dwell in it.
8 Let the rivers clap their hands,
Let the mountains sing
together for joy
9 Before the L ord, for He is
coming to judge the earth;
He will judge the world with
righteousness
And the peoples with equity.

PSALM 99

*Praise to the L ord for His
Fidelity to Israel.*

1 The L ord reigns, let the
peoples tremble;
He is enthroned *above* the
cherubim, let the earth shake!
2 The L ord is great in Zion,
And He is exalted above all
the peoples.
3 Let them praise Your great
and awesome name;
Holy is He.
4 The strength of the King loves
¹justice;
You have established equity;
You have executed ¹justice
and righteousness in Jacob.
5 Exalt the L ord our God
And worship at His footstool;

Holy is He.
6 Moses and Aaron were among
His priests,
And Samuel was among those
who called on His name;
They called upon the L ord
and He answered them.
7 He spoke to them in the pillar
of cloud;
They kept His testimonies
And the statute that He gave
them.
8 O L ord our God, You
answered them;
You were a forgiving God to
them,
And *yet* an avenger of their
evil deeds.
9 Exalt the L ord our God
And worship at His holy hill,
For holy is the L ord our God.

PSALM 100

All Men Exhorted to Praise God.
A Psalm for Thanksgiving.

1 Shout joyfully to the L ord, all
the earth.
2 Serve the L ord with gladness;
Come before Him with joyful
singing.
3 Know that the L ord Himself
is God;
It is He who has made us, and
²not we ourselves;
We are His people and the
sheep of His pasture.
4 Enter His gates with
thanksgiving
And His courts with praise.
Give thanks to Him, bless His
name.
5 For the L ord is good;
His lovingkindness is
everlasting

---

1. Or *judgment* 2. Some mss read *His we are*

And His faithfulness to all
generations.

PSALM 101

*The Psalmist's Profession of
Uprightness.*
A Psalm of David.

1 I will sing of lovingkindness
  and justice,
  To You, O LORD, I will sing
  praises.
2 I will give heed to the
  ¹blameless way.
  When will You come to me?
  I will walk within my house in
  the integrity of my heart.
3 I will set no worthless thing
  before my eyes;
  I hate the work of those who
  fall away;
  It shall not fasten its grip on
  me.
4 A perverse heart shall depart
  from me;
  I will know no evil.
5 Whoever secretly slanders his
  neighbor, him I will destroy;
  No one who has a haughty
  look and an arrogant heart
  will I endure.
6 My eyes shall be upon the
  faithful of the land, that they
  may dwell with me;
  He who walks in a ²blameless
  way is the one who will
  minister to me.
7 He who practices deceit shall
  not dwell within my house;
  He who speaks falsehood shall
  not maintain his position
  before me.
8 Every morning I will ³destroy
  all the wicked of the land,
  So as to cut off from the city of

the LORD all those who do
iniquity.

PSALM 102

*Prayer of an Afflicted Man for
Mercy on Himself and on Zion.*
A Prayer of the Afflicted when he
  is faint and pours out his
  complaint before the LORD.

1 Hear my prayer, O LORD!
  And let my cry for help come
  to You.
2 Do not hide Your face from
  me in the day of my distress;
  Incline Your ear to me;
  In the day when I call answer
  me quickly.
3 For my days have been
  consumed in smoke,
  And my bones have been
  scorched like a hearth.
4 My heart has been smitten like
  grass and has withered away,
  Indeed, I forget to eat my
  bread.
5 Because of the loudness of my
  groaning
  My bones cling to my flesh.
6 I resemble a pelican of the
  wilderness;
  I have become like an owl of
  the waste places.
7 I lie awake,
  I have become like a lonely
  bird on a housetop.
8 My enemies have reproached
  me all day long;
  Those who deride me have
  used my *name* as a curse.
9 For I have eaten ashes like
  bread
  And mingled my drink with
  weeping
10 Because of Your indignation
  and Your wrath,

---

1. Or *way of integrity* 2. Or *way of integrity* 3. Or *silence*

For You have lifted me up and
cast me away.

11 My days are like a lengthened
shadow,
And I wither away like grass.

12 But You, O LORD, abide
forever,
And Your name to all
generations.

13 You will arise *and* have
compassion on Zion;
For it is time to be gracious to
her,
For the appointed time has
come.

14 Surely Your servants find
pleasure in her stones
And feel pity for her dust.

15 So the nations will fear the
name of the LORD
And all the kings of the earth
Your glory.

16 For the LORD has built up
Zion;
He has appeared in His glory.

17 He has regarded the prayer of
the destitute
And has not despised their
prayer.

18 This will be written for the
generation to come,
That a people yet to be created
may praise the LORD.

19 For He looked down from His
holy height;
From heaven the LORD gazed
upon the earth,

20 To hear the groaning of the
prisoner,
To set free those who were
doomed to death,

21 That *men* may tell of the name
of the LORD in Zion
And His praise in Jerusalem,

22 When the peoples are
gathered together,

And the kingdoms, to serve
the LORD.

23 He has weakened my strength
in the way;
He has shortened my days.

24 I say, "O my God, do not take
me away in the midst of my
days,
Your years are throughout all
generations.

25 "Of old You founded the earth,
And the heavens are the work
of Your hands.

26 "Even they will perish, but You
endure;
And all of them will wear out
like a garment;
Like clothing You will change
them and they will be
changed.

27 "But You are the same,
And Your years will not come
to an end.

28 "The children of Your servants
will continue,
And their descendants will be
established before You."

PSALM 103

*Praise for the LORD's Mercies.
A Psalm of David.*

1 Bless the LORD, O my soul,
And all that is within me, *bless*
His holy name.

2 Bless the LORD, O my soul,
And forget none of His
benefits;

3 Who pardons all your
iniquities,
Who heals all your diseases;

4 Who redeems your life from
the pit,
Who crowns you with
lovingkindness and
compassion;

5 Who satisfies your years with
good things,

So that your youth is renewed
like the eagle.

6 The LORD performs righteous
deeds
And judgments for all who are
oppressed.

7 He made known His ways to
Moses,
His acts to the sons of Israel.

8 The LORD is compassionate
and gracious,
Slow to anger and abounding
in lovingkindness.

9 He will not always strive *with
us*,
Nor will He keep *His anger*
forever.

10 He has not dealt with us
according to our sins,
Nor rewarded us according to
our iniquities.

11 For as high as the heavens are
above the earth,
So great is His lovingkindness
toward those who [1]fear Him.

12 As far as the east is from the
west,
So far has He removed our
transgressions from us.

13 Just as a father has
compassion on *his* children,
So the LORD has compassion
on those who fear Him.

14 For He Himself knows [2]our
frame;
He is mindful that we are *but*
dust.

15 As for man, his days are like
grass;
As a flower of the field, so he
flourishes.

16 When the wind has passed
over it, it is no more,
And its place acknowledges it
no longer.

17 But the lovingkindness of the
LORD is from everlasting to
everlasting on those who [3]fear
Him,
And His righteousness to
children's children,

18 To those who keep His
covenant
And remember His precepts to
do them.

19 The LORD has established His
throne in the heavens,
And His [4]sovereignty rules
over all.

20 Bless the LORD, you His
angels,
Mighty in strength, who
perform His word,
Obeying the voice of His word!

21 Bless the LORD, all you His
hosts,
You who serve Him, doing His
will.

22 Bless the LORD, all you works
of His,
In all places of His dominion;
Bless the LORD, O my soul!

PSALM 104

*The LORD's Care over
All His Works.*

1 Bless the LORD, O my soul!
O LORD my God, You are very
great;
You are clothed with splendor
and majesty,

2 Covering Yourself with light
as with a cloak,
Stretching out heaven like a
tent curtain.

3 [5]He lays the beams of His
upper chambers in the
waters;
He makes the clouds His
chariot;

---

1. Or *revere* 2. I.e. what we are made of 3. Or *revere* 4. Or *kingdom* 5. Lit *The one who*

87

He walks upon the wings of
the wind;

4 He makes [1]the winds His
messengers,
[2]Flaming fire His ministers.

5 He established the earth upon
its foundations,
So that it will not [3]totter
forever and ever.

6 You covered it with the deep
as with a garment;
The waters were standing
above the mountains.

7 At Your rebuke they fled,
At the sound of Your thunder
they hurried away.

8 The mountains rose; the
valleys sank down
To the place which You
established for them.

9 You set a boundary that they
may not pass over,
So that they will not return to
cover the earth.

10 He sends forth springs in the
valleys;
They flow between the
mountains;

11 They give drink to every beast
of the field;
The wild donkeys quench
their thirst.

12 Beside them the birds of the
heavens dwell;
They lift up *their* voices
among the branches.

13 He waters the mountains from
His upper chambers;
The earth is satisfied with the
fruit of His works.

14 He causes the grass to grow
for the cattle,
And vegetation for the labor of
man,

So that he may bring forth
food from the earth,

15 And wine which makes man's
heart glad,
So that he may make *his* face
glisten with oil,
And food which sustains
man's heart.

16 The trees of the LORD drink
their fill,
The cedars of Lebanon which
He planted,

17 Where the birds build their
nests,
And the stork, whose home is
the fir trees.

18 The high mountains are for
the wild goats;
The cliffs are a refuge for the
shephanim.

19 He made the moon for the
seasons;
The sun knows the place of its
setting.

20 You appoint darkness and it
becomes night,
In which all the beasts of the
forest prowl about.

21 The young lions roar after
their prey
And seek their food from God.

22 *When* the sun rises they
withdraw
And lie down in their dens.

23 Man goes forth to his work
And to his labor until evening.

24 O LORD, how many are Your
works!
In wisdom You have made
them all;
The earth is full of Your
[4]possessions.

25 There is the sea, great and
broad,

---

1. Or *His angels, spirits* 2. Or *His ministers flames of fire* 3. Or *move out of place*
4. Or *creatures*

In which are swarms without
number,
Animals both small and great.

26 There the ships move along,
And ¹Leviathan, which You
have formed to sport in it.

27 They all wait for You
To give them their food in
²due season.

28 You give to them, they gather
it up;
You open Your hand, they are
satisfied with good.

29 You hide Your face, they are
dismayed;
You take away their ³spirit,
they expire
And return to their dust.

30 You send forth Your ⁴Spirit,
they are created;
And You renew the face of the
ground.

31 Let the glory of the LORD
endure forever;
Let the LORD be glad in His
works;

32 He looks at the earth, and it
trembles;
He touches the mountains,
and they smoke.

33 I will sing to the LORD as long
as I live;
I will sing praise to my God
while I have my being.

34 Let my meditation be pleasing
to Him;
As for me, I shall be glad in
the LORD.

35 Let sinners be consumed from
the earth
And let the wicked be no
more.
Bless the LORD, O my soul.
Praise the LORD!

PSALM 105

*The LORD's Wonderful Works
in Behalf of Israel.*

1 Oh give thanks to the LORD,
call upon His name;
Make known His deeds among
the peoples.

2 Sing to Him, sing praises to
Him;
⁵Speak of all His wonders.

3 Glory in His holy name;
Let the heart of those who
seek the LORD be glad.

4 Seek the LORD and His
strength;
Seek His face continually.

5 Remember His wonders which
He has done,
His marvels and the
judgments uttered by His
mouth,

6 O seed of Abraham, His
servant,
O sons of Jacob, His chosen
ones!

7 He is the LORD our God;
His judgments are in all the
earth.

8 He has remembered His
covenant forever,
The word which He
commanded to a thousand
generations,

9 *The covenant* which He made
with Abraham,
And His oath to Isaac.

10 Then He confirmed it to Jacob
for a statute,
To Israel as an everlasting
covenant,

11 Saying, "To you I will give the
land of Canaan
As the portion of your
inheritance,"

1. Or *a sea monster* 2. Lit *its appointed time* 3. Or *breath* 4. Or *breath*
5. Or *Meditate on*

12 When they were only a few
   men in number,
      Very few, and strangers in it.
13 And they wandered about
   from nation to nation,
      From *one* kingdom to another
      people.
14 He permitted no man to
   oppress them,
      And He reproved kings for
      their sakes:
15 "Do not touch My anointed
   ones,
      And do My prophets no
      harm."
16 And He called for a famine
   upon the land;
      He broke the whole staff of
      bread.
17 He sent a man before them,
   Joseph, *who* was sold as a
   slave.
18 They afflicted his feet with
   fetters,
      He himself was laid in irons;
19 Until the time that his word
   came to pass,
      The word of the LORD tested
      him.
20 The king sent and released
   him,
      The ruler of peoples, and set
      him free.
21 He made him lord of his house
   And ruler over all his
   possessions,
22 To imprison his princes at
   will,
      That he might teach his elders
      wisdom.
23 Israel also came into Egypt;
      Thus Jacob sojourned in the
      land of Ham.
24 And He caused His people to
   be very fruitful,
      And made them stronger than
      their adversaries.

25 He turned their heart to hate
   His people,
      To deal craftily with His
      servants.
26 He sent Moses His servant,
      And Aaron, whom He had
      chosen.
27 They performed His wondrous
   acts among them,
      And miracles in the land of
      Ham.
28 He sent darkness and made *it*
   dark;
      And they did not rebel against
      His words.
29 He turned their waters into
   blood
      And caused their fish to die.
30 Their land swarmed with
   frogs
      Even in the chambers of their
      kings.
31 He spoke, and there came a
   swarm of flies
      And gnats in all their territory.
32 He gave them hail for rain,
      And flaming fire in their land.
33 He struck down their vines
   also and their fig trees,
      And shattered the trees of
      their territory.
34 He spoke, and locusts came,
      And young locusts, even
      without number,
35 And ate up all vegetation in
   their land,
      And ate up the fruit of their
      ground.
36 He also struck down all the
   firstborn in their land,
      The first fruits of all their
      vigor.
37 Then He brought them out
   with silver and gold,
      And among His tribes there
      was not one who stumbled.

38 Egypt was glad when they
departed,
For the dread of them had
fallen upon them.
39 He spread a cloud for a
¹covering,
And fire to illumine by night.
40 They asked, and He brought
quail,
And satisfied them with the
bread of heaven.
41 He opened the rock and water
flowed out;
It ran in the dry places *like* a
river.
42 For He remembered His holy
word
With Abraham His servant;
43 And He brought forth His
people with joy,
His chosen ones with a joyful
shout.
44 He gave them also the lands of
the nations,
That they might take
possession of *the fruit of* the
peoples' labor,
45 So that they might keep His
statutes
And observe His laws,
Praise the LORD!

PSALM 106

*Israel's Rebelliousness and the
LORD'S Deliverances.*

1 Praise the LORD!
Oh give thanks to the LORD,
for He is good;
For His lovingkindness is
everlasting.
2 Who can speak of the mighty
deeds of the LORD,
Or can show forth all His
praise?
3 How blessed are those who
keep justice,

Who practice righteousness at
all times!
4 Remember me, O LORD, in
Your favor toward Your
people;
Visit me with Your salvation,
5 That I may see the prosperity
of Your chosen ones,
That I may rejoice in the
gladness of Your nation,
That I may glory with Your
²inheritance.
6 We have sinned like our
fathers,
We have committed iniquity,
we have behaved wickedly.
7 Our fathers in Egypt did not
understand Your wonders;
They did not remember Your
abundant kindnesses,
But rebelled by the sea, at the
³Red Sea.
8 Nevertheless He saved them
for the sake of His name,
That He might make His
power known.
9 Thus He rebuked the ⁴Red Sea
and it dried up,
And He led them through the
deeps, as through the
wilderness.
10 So He saved them from the
hand of the one who hated
them,
And redeemed them from the
hand of the enemy.
11 The waters covered their
adversaries;
Not one of them was left.
12 Then they believed His words;
They sang His praise.
13 They quickly forgot His
works;
They did not wait for His
counsel,

1. Or *curtain* 2. I.e. people 3. Lit *Sea of Reeds* 4. Lit *Sea of Reeds*

14 But craved intensely in the
   wilderness,
   And tempted God in the
   desert.
15 So He gave them their request,
   But sent a wasting disease
   among them.
16 When they became envious of
   Moses in the camp,
   And of Aaron, the holy one of
   the LORD,
17 The earth opened and
   swallowed up Dathan,
   And engulfed the company of
   Abiram.
18 And a fire blazed up in their
   company;
   The flame consumed the
   wicked.
19 They made a calf in Horeb
   And worshiped a molten
   image.
20 Thus they exchanged their
   glory
   For the image of an ox that
   eats grass.
21 They forgot God their Savior,
   Who had done great things in
   Egypt,
22 Wonders in the land of Ham
   And awesome things by the
   ¹Red Sea.
23 Therefore He said that He
   would destroy them,
   Had not Moses His chosen one
   stood in the breach before
   Him,
   To turn away His wrath from
   destroying *them.*
24 Then they despised the
   pleasant land;
   They did not believe in His
   word,
25 But grumbled in their tents;
   They did not listen to the voice
   of the LORD.

26 Therefore He swore to them
   That He would cast them
   down in the wilderness,
27 And that He would cast their
   seed among the nations
   And scatter them in the lands.
28 They joined themselves also to
   Baal-peor,
   And ate sacrifices offered to
   the dead.
29 Thus they provoked *Him* to
   anger with their deeds,
   And the plague broke out
   among them.
30 Then Phinehas stood up and
   interposed,
   And so the plague was stayed.
31 And it was reckoned to him
   for righteousness,
   To all generations forever.
32 They also provoked *Him* to
   wrath at the waters of
   ²Meribah,
   So that it went hard with
   Moses on their account;
33 Because they were rebellious
   against His Spirit,
   He spoke rashly with his lips.
34 They did not destroy the
   peoples,
   As the LORD commanded
   them,
35 But they mingled with the
   nations
   And learned their practices,
36 And served their idols,
   Which became a snare to
   them.
37 They even sacrificed their sons
   and their daughters to the
   demons,
38 And shed innocent blood,
   The blood of their sons and
   their daughters,

1. Lit *Sea of Reeds* 2. Lit *strife*

Whom they sacrificed to the
idols of Canaan;
And the land was polluted
with the blood.

39 Thus they became unclean in
their practices,
And played the harlot in their
deeds.

40 Therefore the anger of the
Lord was kindled against His
people
And He abhorred His
inheritance.

41 Then He gave them into the
hand of the nations,
And those who hated them
ruled over them.

42 Their enemies also oppressed
them,
And they were subdued under
their power.

43 Many times He would deliver
them;
They, however, were rebellious
in their counsel,
And so sank down in their
iniquity.

44 Nevertheless He looked upon
their distress
When He heard their cry;

45 And He remembered His
covenant for their sake,
And relented according to the
greatness of His
lovingkindness.

46 He also made them *objects* of
compassion
In the presence of all their
captors.

47 Save us, O Lord our God,
And gather us from among the
nations,
To give thanks to Your holy
name
And glory in Your praise.

48 Blessed be the Lord, the God
of Israel,

From everlasting even to
everlasting.
And let all the people say,
"Amen."
Praise the Lord!

BOOK 5
PSALM 107

*The Lord Delivers Men from
Manifold Troubles.*

1 Oh give thanks to the Lord,
for He is good,
For His lovingkindness is
everlasting.

2 Let the redeemed of the Lord
say *so*,
Whom He has redeemed from
the hand of the adversary

3 And gathered from the lands,
From the east and from the
west,
From the north and from the
south.

4 They wandered in the
wilderness in a desert region;
They did not find a way to an
inhabited city.

5 *They were* hungry and thirsty;
Their soul fainted within
them.

6 Then they cried out to the
Lord in their trouble;
He delivered them out of their
distresses.

7 He led them also by a straight
way,
To go to an inhabited city.

8 Let them give thanks to the
Lord for His lovingkindness,
And for His wonders to the
sons of men!

9 For He has satisfied the thirsty
soul,
And the hungry soul He has
filled with what is good.

10 There were those who dwelt in

darkness and in the shadow
of death,
Prisoners in misery and
chains,

11 Because they had rebelled
against the words of God
And spurned the counsel of
the Most High.

12 Therefore He humbled their
heart with labor;
They stumbled and there was
none to help.

13 Then they cried out to the
LORD in their trouble;
He saved them out of their
distresses.

14 He brought them out of
darkness and the shadow of
death
And broke their bands apart.

15 Let them give thanks to the
LORD for His lovingkindness,
And for His wonders to the
sons of men!

16 For He has shattered gates of
bronze
And cut bars of iron asunder.

17 Fools, because of their
rebellious way,
And because of their
iniquities, were afflicted.

18 Their soul abhorred all kinds
of food,
And they drew near to the
gates of death.

19 Then they cried out to the
LORD in their trouble;
He saved them out of their
distresses.

20 He sent His word and healed
them,
And delivered *them* from their
[1]destructions.

21 Let them give thanks to the
LORD for His lovingkindness,

And for His wonders to the
sons of men!

22 Let them also offer sacrifices
of thanksgiving,
And tell of His works with
joyful singing.

23 Those who go down to the sea
in ships,
Who do business on great
waters;

24 They have seen the works of
the LORD,
And His wonders in the deep.

25 For He spoke and raised up a
stormy wind,
Which lifted up the waves of
the sea.

26 They rose up to the heavens,
they went down to the
depths;
Their soul melted away in
their misery.

27 They reeled and staggered like
a drunken man,
And [2]were at their wits' end.

28 Then they cried to the LORD in
their trouble,
And He brought them out of
their distresses.

29 He caused the storm to be still,
So that the waves of the sea
were hushed.

30 Then they were glad because
they were quiet,
So He guided them to their
desired haven.

31 Let them give thanks to the
LORD for His lovingkindness,
And for His wonders to the
sons of men!

32 Let them extol Him also in the
congregation of the people,
And praise Him at the seat of
the elders.

33 He [3]changes rivers into a
wilderness

1. Or *pits* 2. Lit *all their wisdom was swallowed up* 3. Or *turns*

And springs of water into a
thirsty ground;

34 A fruitful land into a salt
waste,
Because of the wickedness of
those who dwell in it.

35 He changes a wilderness into a
pool of water
And a dry land into springs of
water;

36 And there He makes the
hungry to dwell,
So that they may establish an
inhabited city,

37 And sow fields and plant
vineyards,
And gather a fruitful harvest.

38 Also He blesses them and they
multiply greatly,
And He does not let their
cattle decrease.

39 When they are diminished
and bowed down
Through oppression, misery
and sorrow,

40 He pours contempt upon
princes
And makes them wander in a
pathless waste.

41 But He sets the needy securely
on high away from affliction,
And makes *his* families like a
flock.

42 The upright see it and are
glad;
But all unrighteousness shuts
its mouth.

43 Who is wise? Let him give
heed to these things,
And consider the
lovingkindnesses of the
LORD.

1. Or *sanctuary*   2. Or *lawgiver*

PSALM 108

*God Praised and Supplicated to
Give Victory.*
A Song, a Psalm of David.

1 My heart is steadfast, O God;
I will sing, I will sing praises,
even with my soul.

2 Awake, harp and lyre;
I will awaken the dawn!

3 I will give thanks to You, O
LORD, among the peoples,
And I will sing praises to You
among the nations.

4 For Your lovingkindness is
great above the heavens,
And Your truth *reaches* to the
skies.

5 Be exalted, O God, above the
heavens,
And Your glory above all the
earth.

6 That Your beloved may be
delivered,
Save with Your right hand,
and answer me!

7 God has spoken in His
[1]holiness:
"I will exult, I will portion out
Shechem
And measure out the valley of
Succoth.

8 "Gilead is Mine, Manasseh is
Mine;
Ephraim also is the helmet of
My head;
Judah is My [2]scepter.

9 "Moab is My washbowl;
Over Edom I shall throw My
shoe;
Over Philistia I will shout
aloud."

10 Who will bring me into the
besieged city?
Who will lead me to Edom?

11 Have not You Yourself, O
God, rejected us?
And will You not go forth
with our armies, O God?
12 Oh give us help against the
adversary,
For deliverance by man is in
vain.
13 Through God we will do
valiantly,
And it is He who shall tread
down our adversaries.

PSALM 109

*Vengeance Invoked
upon Adversaries.*
For the choir director.
A Psalm of David.

1 O God of my praise,
Do not be silent!
2 For they have opened the
wicked and deceitful mouth
against me;
They have spoken against me
with a lying tongue.
3 They have also surrounded me
with words of hatred,
And fought against me
without cause.
4 In return for my love they act
as my accusers;
But I am *in* prayer.
5 Thus they have repaid me evil
for good
And hatred for my love.
6 Appoint a wicked man over
him,
And let an accuser stand at his
right hand.
7 When he is judged, let him
come forth guilty,
And let his prayer become sin.
8 Let his days be few;
Let another take his office.
9 Let his children be fatherless
And his wife a widow.

10 Let his children wander about
and beg;
And let them seek *sustenance*
far from their ruined homes.
11 Let the creditor seize all that
he has,
And let strangers plunder the
product of his labor.
12 Let there be none to extend
lovingkindness to him,
Nor any to be gracious to his
fatherless children.
13 Let his posterity be cut off;
In a following generation let
their name be blotted out.
14 Let the iniquity of his fathers
be remembered before the
LORD,
And do not let the sin of his
mother be blotted out.
15 Let them be before the LORD
continually,
That He may cut off their
memory from the earth;
16 Because he did not remember
to show lovingkindness,
But persecuted the afflicted
and needy man,
And the despondent in heart,
to put *them* to death.
17 He also loved cursing, so it
came to him;
And he did not delight in
blessing, so it was far from
him.
18 But he clothed himself with
cursing as with his garment,
And it entered into his body
like water
And like oil into his bones.
19 Let it be to him as a garment
with which he covers himself,
And for a belt with which he
constantly girds himself.
20 Let this be the reward of my
accusers from the LORD,

And of those who speak evil
  against my soul.
21 But You, O GOD, the Lord,
  deal *kindly* with me for Your
  name's sake;
  Because Your lovingkindness
  is good, deliver me;
22 For I am afflicted and needy,
  And my heart is wounded
  within me.
23 I am passing like a shadow
  when it lengthens;
  I am shaken off like the locust.
24 My knees are weak from
  fasting,
  And my flesh has grown lean,
  without fatness.
25 I also have become a reproach
  to them;
  When they see me, they wag
  their head.
26 Help me, O LORD my God;
  Save me according to Your
  lovingkindness.
27 And let them know that this is
  Your hand;
  You, LORD, have done it.
28 Let them curse, but You bless;
  When they arise, they shall be
  ashamed,
  But Your servant shall be
  glad.
29 Let my accusers be clothed
  with dishonor,
  And let them cover themselves
  with their own shame as with
  a robe.
30 With my mouth I will give
  thanks abundantly to the
  LORD;
  And in the midst of many I
  will praise Him.
31 For He stands at the right
  hand of the needy,
  To save him from those who
  judge his soul.

PSALM 110

*The LORD Gives Dominion
to the King.*
A Psalm of David.

1 The LORD says to my Lord:
  "Sit at My right hand
  Until I make Your enemies a
  footstool for Your feet."
2 The LORD will stretch forth
  Your strong scepter from
  Zion, *saying,*
  "Rule in the midst of Your
  enemies."
3 Your people will volunteer
  freely in the day of Your
  power;
  In holy array, from the womb
  of the dawn,
  Your youth are to You *as* the
  dew.
4 The LORD has sworn and will
  not change His mind,
  "You are a priest forever
  According to the order of
  Melchizedek."
5 The Lord is at Your right
  hand;
  He will shatter kings in the
  day of His wrath.
6 He will judge among the
  nations,
  He will fill *them* with corpses,
  He will shatter the chief men
  over a broad country.
7 He will drink from the brook
  by the wayside;
  Therefore He will lift up *His*
  head.

PSALM 111

*The LORD Praised for
His Goodness.*

1 Praise the LORD!
  I will give thanks to the LORD
  with all *my* heart,

In the company of the upright
and in the assembly.

2 Great are the works of the
Lord;
They are studied by all who
delight in them.

3 Splendid and majestic is His
work,
And His righteousness
endures forever.

4 He has made His wonders to
be remembered;
The Lord is gracious and
compassionate.

5 He has given food to those
who ¹fear Him;
He will remember His
covenant forever.

6 He has made known to His
people the power of His
works,
In giving them the heritage of
the nations.

7 The works of His hands are
truth and justice;
All His precepts are sure.

8 They are upheld forever and
ever;
They are performed in truth
and uprightness.

9 He has sent redemption to His
people;
He has ordained His covenant
forever;

Holy and awesome is His
name.

10 The ²fear of the Lord is the
beginning of wisdom;
A good understanding have all
those who do *His
commandments;*

His praise endures forever.

PSALM 112

*Prosperity of the One
Who Fears the Lord.*

1 Praise the Lord!
How blessed is the man who
fears the Lord,
Who greatly delights in His
commandments.

2 His ³descendants will be
mighty on earth;
The generation of the upright
will be blessed.

3 Wealth and riches are in his
house,
And his righteousness endures
forever.

4 Light arises in the darkness
for the upright;
He is gracious and
compassionate and righteous.

5 It is well with the man who is
gracious and lends;
He will maintain his cause in
judgment.

6 For he will never be shaken;
The righteous will be
remembered forever.

7 He will not fear evil tidings;
His heart is steadfast, trusting
in the Lord.

8 His heart is upheld, he will not
fear,
Until he looks *with
satisfaction* on his
adversaries.

9 He has given freely to the
poor,
His righteousness endures
forever;
His horn will be exalted in
honor.

10 The wicked will see it and be
vexed,
He will gnash his teeth and
melt away;

---

1. Or *revere* 2. Or *reverence for* 3. Lit *seed*

The desire of the wicked will
perish.

PSALM 113

The LORD Exalts the Humble.

1 Praise the LORD!
   Praise, O servants of the LORD,
   Praise the name of the LORD.
2 Blessed be the name of the
   LORD
   From this time forth and
   forever.
3 From the rising of the sun to
   its setting
   The name of the LORD is to be
   praised.
4 The LORD is high above all
   nations;
   His glory is above the heavens.
5 Who is like the LORD our God,
   Who is enthroned on high,
6 Who humbles Himself to
   behold
   The things that are in heaven
   and in the earth?
7 He raises the poor from the
   dust
   And lifts the needy from the
   ash heap,
8 To make *them* sit with
   princes,
   With the princes of His
   people.
9 He makes the barren woman
   abide in the house
   As a joyful mother of children.
   Praise the LORD!

PSALM 114

*God's Deliverance of
Israel from Egypt.*

1 When Israel went forth from
   Egypt,
   The house of Jacob from a
   people of strange language,
2 Judah became His sanctuary,

Israel, His dominion.
3 The sea looked and fled;
   The Jordan turned back.
4 The mountains skipped like
   rams,
   The hills, like lambs.
5 What ails you, O sea, that you
   flee?
   O Jordan, that you turn back?
6 O mountains, that you skip
   like rams?
   O hills, like lambs?
7 Tremble, O earth, before the
   Lord,
   Before the God of Jacob,
8 Who turned the rock into a
   pool of water,
   The flint into a fountain of
   water.

PSALM 115

*Heathen Idols Contrasted
with the LORD.*

1 Not to us, O LORD, not to us,
   But to Your name give glory
   Because of Your
   lovingkindness, because of
   Your truth.
2 Why should the nations say,
   "Where, now, is their God?"
3 But our God is in the heavens;
   He does whatever He pleases.
4 Their idols are silver and gold,
   The work of man's hands.
5 They have mouths, but they
   cannot speak;
   They have eyes, but they
   cannot see;
6 They have ears, but they
   cannot hear;
   They have noses, but they
   cannot smell;
7 They have hands, but they
   cannot feel;
   They have feet, but they
   cannot walk;

They cannot make a sound
with their throat.

8 Those who make them will
become like them,
Everyone who trusts in them.

9 O Israel, trust in the Lord;
He is their help and their
shield.

10 O house of Aaron, trust in the
Lord;
He is their help and their
shield.

11 You who ¹fear the Lord, trust
in the Lord;
He is their help and their
shield.

12 The Lord has been mindful of
us; He will bless *us;*
He will bless the house of
Israel;
He will bless the house of
Aaron.

13 He will bless those who ²fear
the Lord,
The small together with the
great.

14 May the Lord give you
increase,
You and your children.

15 May you be blessed of the
Lord,
Maker of heaven and earth.

16 The heavens are the heavens
of the Lord,
But the earth He has given to
the sons of men.

17 The dead do not praise the
Lord,
Nor *do* any who go down into
silence;

18 But as for us, we will bless the
Lord
From this time forth and
forever.
Praise the Lord!

PSALM 116

*Thanksgiving for Deliverance
from Death.*

1 I love the Lord, because He
hears
My voice *and* my
supplications.

2 Because He has inclined His
ear to me,
Therefore I shall call *upon
Him* as long as I live.

3 The cords of death
encompassed me
And the terrors of Sheol came
upon me;
I found distress and sorrow.

4 Then I called upon the name
of the Lord:
"O Lord, I beseech You, save
my life!"

5 Gracious is the Lord, and
righteous;
Yes, our God is
compassionate.

6 The Lord preserves the
simple;
I was brought low, and He
saved me.

7 Return to your rest, O my
soul,
For the Lord has dealt
bountifully with you.

8 For You have rescued my soul
from death,
My eyes from tears,
My feet from stumbling.

9 I shall walk before the Lord
In the land of the living.

10 I believed when I said,
"I am greatly afflicted."

11 I said in my alarm,
"All men are liars."

12 What shall I render to the
Lord

For all His benefits toward me?

13 I shall lift up the cup of salvation
And call upon the name of the LORD.

14 I shall pay my vows to the LORD,
Oh *may it be* in the presence of all His people.

15 Precious in the sight of the LORD
Is the death of His godly ones.

16 O LORD, surely I am Your servant,
I am Your servant, the son of Your handmaid,
You have loosed my bonds.

17 To You I shall offer a sacrifice of thanksgiving,
And call upon the name of the LORD.

18 I shall pay my vows to the LORD,
Oh *may it be* in the presence of all His people,

19 In the courts of the LORD's house,
In the midst of you, O Jerusalem.
Praise the LORD!

PSALM 117

A Psalm of Praise.

1 Praise the LORD, all nations;
Laud Him, all peoples!

2 For His lovingkindness [1]is great toward us,
And the truth of the LORD is everlasting.
Praise the LORD!

PSALM 118

Thanksgiving for the LORD's Saving Goodness.

1 Give thanks to the LORD, for He is good;
For His lovingkindness is everlasting.

2 Oh let Israel say,
"His lovingkindness is everlasting."

3 Oh let the house of Aaron say,
"His lovingkindness is everlasting."

4 Oh let those who [2]fear the LORD say,
"His lovingkindness is everlasting."

5 From *my* distress I called upon the LORD;
The LORD answered me *and set me* in a large place.

6 The LORD is for me; I will not fear;
What can man do to me?

7 The LORD is for me among those who help me;
Therefore I will look *with satisfaction* on those who hate me.

8 It is better to take refuge in the LORD
Than to trust in man.

9 It is better to take refuge in the LORD
Than to trust in princes.

10 All nations surrounded me;
In the name of the LORD I will surely cut them off.

11 They surrounded me, yes, they surrounded me;
In the name of the LORD I will surely cut them off.

12 They surrounded me like bees;
They were extinguished as a fire of thorns;

---

1. Lit *prevails over us* 2. Or *revere*

In the name of the LORD I will
surely cut them off.
13 You pushed me violently so
that I was falling,
But the LORD helped me.
14 The LORD is my strength and
song,
And He has become my
salvation.
15 The sound of joyful shouting
and salvation is in the tents of
the righteous;
The right hand of the LORD
does valiantly.
16 The right hand of the LORD is
exalted;
The right hand of the LORD
does valiantly.
17 I will not die, but live,
And tell of the works of the
LORD.
18 The LORD has disciplined me
severely,
But He has not given me over
to death.
19 Open to me the gates of
righteousness;
I shall enter through them, I
shall give thanks to the LORD.
20 This is the gate of the LORD;
The righteous will enter
through it.
21 I shall give thanks to You, for
You have answered me,
And You have become my
salvation.
22 The stone which the builders
rejected
Has become the chief corner
stone.
23 This is ¹the LORD's doing;
It is marvelous in our eyes.
24 This is the day which the LORD
has made;
Let us rejoice and be glad in it.

25 O LORD, do save, we beseech
You;
O LORD, we beseech You, do
send prosperity!
26 Blessed is the one who comes
in the name of the LORD;
We have blessed you from the
house of the LORD.
27 The LORD is God, and He has
given us light;
Bind the festival sacrifice with
cords to the horns of the
altar.
28 You are my God, and I give
thanks to You;
You are my God, I extol You.
29 Give thanks to the LORD, for
He is good;
For His lovingkindness is
everlasting.

PSALM 119

*Meditations and Prayers
Relating to the Law of God.*

Aleph.

1 How blessed are those whose
way is ²blameless,
Who walk in the law of the
LORD.
2 How blessed are those who
observe His testimonies,
Who seek Him with all *their*
heart.
3 They also do no
unrighteousness;
They walk in His ways.
4 You have ordained Your
precepts,
That we should keep *them*
diligently.
5 Oh that my ways may be
established
To keep Your statutes!
6 Then I shall not be ashamed

---

1. Lit *from the* LORD 2. Lit *complete; or having integrity*

When I look upon all Your
commandments.

7 I shall give thanks to You with
uprightness of heart,
When I learn Your righteous
judgments.

8 I shall keep Your statutes;
Do not forsake me utterly!

Beth.

9 How can a young man keep
his way pure?
By keeping *it* according to
Your word.

10 With all my heart I have
sought You;
Do not let me wander from
Your commandments.

11 Your word I have treasured in
my heart,
That I may not sin against
You.

12 Blessed are You, O LORD;
Teach me Your statutes.

13 With my lips I have told of
All the ordinances of Your
mouth.

14 I have rejoiced in the way of
Your testimonies,
As much as in all riches.

15 I will meditate on Your
precepts
And regard Your ways.

16 I shall delight in Your
statutes;
I shall not forget Your word.

Gimel.

17 Deal bountifully with Your
servant,
That I may live and keep
Your word.

18 Open my eyes, that I may
behold
Wonderful things from Your
law.

19 I am a stranger in the earth;

Do not hide Your
commandments from me.

20 My soul is crushed with
longing
After Your ordinances at all
times.

21 You rebuke the arrogant, the
cursed,
Who wander from Your
commandments.

22 Take away reproach and
contempt from me,
For I observe Your
testimonies.

23 Even though princes sit *and*
talk against me,
Your servant meditates on
Your statutes.

24 Your testimonies also are my
delight;
They are my counselors.

Daleth.

25 My soul cleaves to the dust;
Revive me according to Your
word.

26 I have told of my ways, and
You have answered me;
Teach me Your statutes.

27 Make me understand the way
of Your precepts,
So I will meditate on Your
wonders.

28 My soul weeps because of
grief;
Strengthen me according to
Your word.

29 Remove the false way from
me,
And graciously grant me Your
law.

30 I have chosen the faithful way;
I have placed Your ordinances
before me.

31 I cling to Your testimonies;
O LORD, do not put me to
shame!

32 I shall run the way of Your
commandments,
For You will enlarge my heart.

He.

33 Teach me, O LORD, the way of
Your statutes,
And I shall observe it to the
end.
34 Give me understanding, that I
may observe Your law
And keep it with all *my* heart.
35 Make me walk in the path of
Your commandments,
For I delight in it.
36 Incline my heart to Your
testimonies
And not to *dishonest* gain.
37 Turn away my eyes from
looking at vanity,
And revive me in Your ways.
38 Establish Your word to Your
servant,
As that which produces
reverence for You.
39 Turn away my reproach
which I dread,
For Your ordinances are good.
40 Behold, I long for Your
precepts;
Revive me through Your
righteousness.

Vav.

41 May Your lovingkindnesses
also come to me, O LORD,
Your salvation according to
Your word;
42 So I will have an answer for
him who reproaches me,
For I trust in Your word.
43 And do not take the word of
truth utterly out of my
mouth,
For I wait for Your
ordinances.

44 So I will keep Your law
continually,
Forever and ever.
45 And I will walk at liberty,
For I seek Your precepts.
46 I will also speak of Your
testimonies before kings
And shall not be ashamed.
47 I shall delight in Your
commandments,
Which I love.
48 And I shall lift up my hands to
Your commandments,
Which I love;
And I will meditate on Your
statutes.

Zayin.

49 Remember the word to Your
servant,
In which You have made me
hope.
50 This is my comfort in my
affliction,
That Your word has revived
me.
51 The arrogant utterly deride
me,
Yet I do not turn aside from
Your law.
52 I have remembered Your
ordinances from ¹old, O
LORD,
And comfort myself.
53 Burning indignation has
seized me because of the
wicked,
Who forsake Your law.
54 Your statutes are my songs
In the house of my pilgrimage.
55 O LORD, I remember Your
name in the night,
And keep Your law.
56 This has become mine,
That I observe Your precepts.

1. Or *everlasting*

Heth.

57 The LORD is my portion;
I have promised to keep Your words.

58 I sought Your favor with all *my* heart;
Be gracious to me according to Your word.

59 I considered my ways
And turned my feet to Your testimonies.

60 I hastened and did not delay
To keep Your commandments.

61 The cords of the wicked have encircled me,
But I have not forgotten Your law.

62 At midnight I shall rise to give thanks to You
Because of Your righteous ordinances.

63 I am a companion of all those who fear You,
And of those who keep Your precepts.

64 The earth is full of Your lovingkindness, O LORD;
Teach me Your statutes.

Teth.

65 You have dealt well with Your servant,
O LORD, according to Your word.

66 Teach me good discernment and knowledge,
For I believe in Your commandments.

67 Before I was afflicted I went astray,
But now I keep Your word.

68 You are good and do good;
Teach me Your statutes.

69 The arrogant ¹have forged a lie against me;

With all *my* heart I will observe Your precepts.

70 Their heart is covered with fat,
But I delight in Your law.

71 It is good for me that I was afflicted,
That I may learn Your statutes.

72 The law of Your mouth is better to me
Than thousands of gold and silver *pieces.*

Yodh.

73 Your hands made me and ²fashioned me;
Give me understanding, that I may learn Your commandments.

74 May those who fear You see me and be glad,
Because I wait for Your word.

75 I know, O LORD, that Your judgments are righteous,
And that in faithfulness You have afflicted me.

76 O may Your lovingkindness comfort me,
According to Your word to Your servant.

77 May Your compassion come to me that I may live,
For Your law is my delight.

78 May the arrogant be ashamed, for they subvert me with a lie;
But I shall meditate on Your precepts.

79 May those who fear You turn to me,
Even those who know Your testimonies.

80 May my heart be blameless in Your statutes,
So that I will not be ashamed.

1. Lit *besmear me with lies* 2. Lit *established*

105

Kaph.

81 My soul languishes for Your
salvation;
I wait for Your word.

82 My eyes fail *with longing* for
Your word,
While I say, "When will You
comfort me?"

83 Though I have become like a
wineskin in the smoke,
I do not forget Your statutes.

84 How many are the days of
Your servant?
When will You execute
judgment on those who
persecute me?

85 The arrogant have dug pits for
me,
Men who are not in accord
with Your law.

86 All Your commandments are
faithful;
They have persecuted me with
a lie; help me!

87 They almost destroyed me on
earth,
But as for me, I did not
forsake Your precepts.

88 Revive me according to Your
lovingkindness,
So that I may keep the
testimony of Your mouth.

Lamedh.

89 Forever, O Lᴏʀᴅ,
Your word ¹is settled in
heaven.

90 Your faithfulness *continues*
throughout all generations;
You established the earth, and
it stands.

91 They stand this day according
to Your ordinances,
For all things are Your
servants.

92 If Your law had not been my
delight,
Then I would have perished in
my affliction.

93 I will never forget Your
precepts,
For by them You have revived
me.

94 I am Yours, save me;
For I have sought Your
precepts.

95 The wicked wait for me to
destroy me;
I shall diligently consider
Your testimonies.

96 I have seen a limit to all
perfection;
Your commandment is
exceedingly broad.

Mem.

97 O how I love Your law!
It is my meditation all the day.

98 Your commandments make
me wiser than my enemies,
For they are ever mine.

99 I have more insight than all
my teachers,
For Your testimonies are my
meditation.

100 I understand more than the
aged,
Because I have observed
Your precepts.

101 I have restrained my feet
from every evil way,
That I may keep Your word.

102 I have not turned aside from
Your ordinances,
For You Yourself have
taught me.

103 How sweet are Your words to
my taste!
Yes, sweeter than honey to
my mouth!

---

1. Lit *stands firm*

104 From Your precepts I get
understanding;
Therefore I hate every false
way.

Nun.

105 Your word is a lamp to my
feet
And a light to my path.
106 I have sworn and I will
confirm it,
That I will keep Your
righteous ordinances.
107 I am exceedingly afflicted;
Revive me, O Lord,
according to Your word.
108 O accept the freewill
offerings of my mouth, O
Lord,
And teach me Your
ordinances.
109 My life is continually [1]in my
hand,
Yet I do not forget Your law.
110 The wicked have laid a snare
for me,
Yet I have not gone astray
from Your precepts.
111 I have inherited Your
testimonies forever,
For they are the joy of my
heart.
112 I have inclined my heart to
perform Your statutes
Forever, *even* to the end.

Samekh.

113 I hate those who are
double-minded,
But I love Your law.
114 You are my hiding place and
my shield;
I wait for Your word.
115 Depart from me, evildoers,
That I may observe the
commandments of my God.

116 Sustain me according to Your
word, that I may live;
And do not let me be
ashamed of my hope.
117 Uphold me that I may be
safe,
That I may have regard for
Your statutes continually.
118 You have rejected all those
who wander from Your
statutes,
For their deceitfulness is
useless.
119 You have removed all the
wicked of the earth *like*
dross;
Therefore I love Your
testimonies.
120 My flesh trembles for fear of
You,
And I am afraid of Your
judgments.

Ayin.

121 I have done justice and
righteousness;
Do not leave me to my
oppressors.
122 Be surety for Your servant
for good;
Do not let the arrogant
oppress me.
123 My eyes fail *with longing* for
Your salvation
And for Your righteous word.
124 Deal with Your servant
according to Your
lovingkindness
And teach me Your statutes.
125 I am Your servant; give me
understanding,
That I may know Your
testimonies.
126 It is time for the Lord to act,
For they have broken Your
law.

---

1. I.e. in danger

127 Therefore I love Your
commandments
Above gold, yes, above fine
gold.
128 Therefore I esteem right all
Your precepts concerning
everything,
I hate every false way.

Pe.

129 Your testimonies are
wonderful;
Therefore my soul observes
them.
130 The unfolding of Your words
gives light;
It gives understanding to the
simple.
131 I opened my mouth wide and
panted,
For I longed for Your
commandments.
132 Turn to me and be gracious
to me,
After Your manner with
those who love Your name.
133 Establish my footsteps in
Your word,
And do not let any iniquity
have dominion over me.
134 Redeem me from the
oppression of man,
That I may keep Your
precepts.
135 Make Your face shine upon
Your servant,
And teach me Your statutes.
136 My eyes shed streams of
water,
Because they do not keep
Your law.

Tsadhe.

137 Righteous are You, O Lord,
And upright are Your
judgments.

138 You have commanded Your
testimonies in righteousness
And exceeding faithfulness.
139 My zeal has consumed me,
Because my adversaries have
forgotten Your words.
140 Your word is very pure,
Therefore Your servant loves
it.
141 I am small and despised,
Yet I do not forget Your
precepts.
142 Your righteousness is an
everlasting righteousness,
And Your law is truth.
143 Trouble and anguish have
come upon me,
Yet Your commandments are
my delight.
144 Your testimonies are
righteous forever;
Give me understanding that I
may live.

Qoph.

145 I cried with all my heart;
answer me, O Lord!
I will observe Your statutes.
146 I cried to You; save me
And I shall keep Your
testimonies.
147 I rise before dawn and cry for
help;
I wait for Your words.
148 My eyes anticipate the night
watches,
That I may meditate on Your
word.
149 Hear my voice according to
Your lovingkindness;
Revive me, O Lord,
according to Your
ordinances.
150 Those who follow after
wickedness draw near;
They are far from Your law.
151 You are near, O Lord,

And all Your commandments
are truth.
152 Of old I have known from
Your testimonies
That You have founded them
forever.

Resh.

153 Look upon my affliction and
rescue me,
For I do not forget Your law.
154 Plead my cause and redeem
me;
Revive me according to Your
word.
155 Salvation is far from the
wicked,
For they do not seek Your
statutes.
156 Great are Your mercies, O
LORD;
Revive me according to Your
ordinances.
157 Many are my persecutors and
my adversaries,
Yet I do not turn aside from
Your testimonies.
158 I behold the treacherous and
loathe *them*,
Because they do not keep
Your word.
159 Consider how I love Your
precepts;
Revive me, O LORD,
according to Your
lovingkindness.
160 The sum of Your word is
truth,
And every one of Your
righteous ordinances is
everlasting.

Shin.

161 Princes persecute me without
cause,
But my heart stands in awe
of Your words.

162 I rejoice at Your word,
As one who finds great spoil.
163 I hate and despise falsehood,
But I love Your law.
164 Seven times a day I praise
You,
Because of Your righteous
ordinances.
165 Those who love Your law
have great peace,
And nothing causes them to
stumble.
166 I hope for Your salvation, O
LORD,
And do Your
commandments.
167 My soul keeps Your
testimonies,
And I love them exceedingly.
168 I keep Your precepts and
Your testimonies,
For all my ways are before
You.

Tav.

169 Let my cry come before You,
O LORD;
Give me understanding
according to Your word.
170 Let my supplication come
before You;
Deliver me according to Your
word.
171 Let my lips utter praise,
For You teach me Your
statutes.
172 Let my tongue sing of Your
word,
For all Your commandments
are righteousness.
173 Let Your hand be ready to
help me,
For I have chosen Your
precepts.
174 I long for Your salvation, O
LORD,
And Your law is my delight.

175 Let my soul live that it may
praise You,
And let Your ordinances help
me.
176 I have gone astray like a lost
sheep; seek Your servant,
For I do not forget Your
commandments.

PSALM 120

*Prayer for Deliverance from the
Treacherous.*
A Song of Ascents.

1 In my trouble I cried to the
LORD,
And He answered me.
2 Deliver my soul, O LORD, from
lying lips,
From a deceitful tongue.
3 What shall be given to you,
and what more shall be done
to you,
You deceitful tongue?
4 Sharp arrows of the warrior,
With the *burning* coals of the
broom tree.
5 Woe is me, for I sojourn in
Meshech,
For I dwell among the tents of
Kedar!
6 Too long has my soul had its
dwelling
With those who hate peace.
7 I am *for* peace, but when I
speak,
They are for war.

PSALM 121

The LORD the Keeper of Israel.
A Song of Ascents.

1 I will lift up my eyes to the
mountains;
From where shall my help
come?
2 My help *comes* from the LORD,

Who made heaven and earth.
3 He will not allow your foot to
slip;
He who keeps you will not
slumber.
4 Behold, He who keeps Israel
Will neither slumber nor sleep.
5 The LORD is your keeper;
The LORD is your shade on
your right hand.
6 The sun will not smite you by
day,
Nor the moon by night.
7 The LORD will ¹protect you
from all evil;
He will keep your soul.
8 The LORD will ²guard your
going out and your coming in
From this time forth and
forever.

PSALM 122

*Prayer for the Peace
of Jerusalem.*
A Song of Ascents, of David.

1 I was glad when they said to
me,
"Let us go to the house of the
LORD."
2 Our feet are standing
Within your gates, O
Jerusalem,
3 Jerusalem, that is built
As a city that is compact
together;
4 To which the tribes go up,
even the tribes of the LORD—
An ordinance for Israel—
To give thanks to the name of
the LORD.
5 For there thrones were set for
judgment,
The thrones of the house of
David.

1. Or *keep* 2. Or *keep*

6 Pray for the peace of
  Jerusalem:
"May they prosper who love
  you.
7"May peace be within your
  walls,
And prosperity within your
  palaces."
8 For the sake of my brothers
  and my friends,
I will now say, "May peace be
  within you."
9 For the sake of the house of
  the LORD our God,
I will seek your good.

PSALM 123

Prayer for the LORD's Help.
A Song of Ascents.

1 To You I lift up my eyes,
  O You who are enthroned in
  the heavens!
2 Behold, as the eyes of servants
  look to the hand of their
  master,
As the eyes of a maid to the
  hand of her mistress,
So our eyes *look* to the LORD
  our God,
Until He is gracious to us.
3 Be gracious to us, O LORD, be
  gracious to us,
For we are greatly filled with
  contempt.
4 Our soul is greatly filled
  With the scoffing of those who
  are at ease,
And with the contempt of the
  proud.

PSALM 124

Praise for Rescue from Enemies.
A Song of Ascents, of David.

1"Had it not been the LORD who
  was on our side,"
Let Israel now say,

2"Had it not been the LORD who
  was on our side
When men rose up against us,
3 Then they would have
  swallowed us alive,
When their anger was kindled
  against us;
4 Then the waters would have
  engulfed us,
The stream would have swept
  over our soul;
5 Then the raging waters would
  have swept over our soul."
6 Blessed be the LORD,
  Who has not given us to be
  torn by their teeth.
7 Our soul has escaped as a bird
  out of the snare of the
  trapper;
The snare is broken and we
  have escaped.
8 Our help is in the name of the
  LORD,
Who made heaven and earth.

PSALM 125

The LORD Surrounds His People.
A Song of Ascents.

1 Those who trust in the LORD
  Are as Mount Zion, which
  cannot be moved but abides
  forever.
2 As the mountains surround
  Jerusalem,
So the LORD surrounds His
  people
From this time forth and
  forever.
3 For the scepter of wickedness
  shall not rest upon the land of
  the righteous,
So that the righteous will not
  put forth their hands to do
  wrong.
4 Do good, O LORD, to those
  who are good

And to those who are upright
in their hearts.
5 But as for those who turn
aside to their crooked ways,
The Lord will lead them away
with the doers of iniquity.
Peace be upon Israel.

PSALM 126

*Thanksgiving for Return
from Captivity.*
A Song of Ascents.

1 When the Lord brought back
the captive ones of Zion,
We were like those who
dream.
2 Then our mouth was filled
with laughter
And our tongue with joyful
shouting;
Then they said among the
nations,
"The Lord has done great
things for them."
3 The Lord has done great
things for us;
We are glad.
4 Restore our captivity, O Lord,
As the streams in the South.
5 Those who sow in tears shall
reap with joyful shouting.
6 He who goes to and fro
weeping, carrying *his* bag of
seed,
Shall indeed come again with
a shout of joy, bringing his
sheaves *with him.*

PSALM 127

Prosperity Comes from the Lord.
A Song of Ascents, of Solomon.

1 Unless the Lord builds the
house,
They labor in vain who build
it;

1. Lit *labor*

Unless the Lord guards the
city,
The watchman keeps awake
in vain.
2 It is vain for you to rise up
early,
To retire late,
To eat the bread of painful
labors;
For He gives to His beloved
even in his sleep.
3 Behold, children are a gift of
the Lord,
The fruit of the womb is a
reward.
4 Like arrows in the hand of a
warrior,
So are the children of one's
youth.
5 How blessed is the man whose
quiver is full of them;
They will not be ashamed
When they speak with their
enemies in the gate.

PSALM 128

*Blessedness of the Fear
of the Lord.*
A Song of Ascents.

1 How blessed is everyone who
fears the Lord,
Who walks in His ways.
2 When you shall eat of the
¹fruit of your hands,
You will be happy and it will
be well with you.
3 Your wife shall be like a
fruitful vine
Within your house,
Your children like olive plants
Around your table.
4 Behold, for thus shall the man
be blessed
Who fears the Lord.
5 The Lord bless you from Zion,

And may you see the
prosperity of Jerusalem all
the days of your life.

6 Indeed, may you see your
children's children.
Peace be upon Israel!

PSALM 129

*Prayer for the Overthrow
of Zion's Enemies.*
A Song of Ascents.

1 "Many times they have
persecuted me from my youth
up,"
Let Israel now say,

2 "Many times they have
persecuted me from my youth
up;
Yet they have not prevailed
against me.

3 "The plowers plowed upon my
back;
They lengthened their
furrows."

4 The LORD is righteous;
He has cut in two the cords of
the wicked.

5 May all who hate Zion
Be put to shame and turned
backward;

6 Let them be like grass upon
the housetops,
Which withers before it grows
up;

7 With which the reaper does
not fill his hand,
Or the binder of sheaves his
bosom;

8 Nor do those who pass by
say,
"The blessing of the LORD be
upon you;
We bless you in the name of
the LORD."

PSALM 130

*Hope in the LORD'S
Forgiving Love.*
A Song of Ascents.

1 Out of the depths I have cried
to You, O LORD.

2 Lord, hear my voice!
Let Your ears be attentive
To the voice of my
supplications.

3 If You, LORD, should mark
iniquities,
O Lord, who could stand?

4 But there is forgiveness with
You,
That You may be feared.

5 I wait for the LORD, my soul
does wait,
And in His word do I hope.

6 My soul *waits* for the Lord
More than the watchmen for
the morning;
Indeed, more than the
watchmen for the morning.

7 O Israel, hope in the LORD;
For with the LORD there is
lovingkindness,
And with Him is abundant
redemption.

8 And He will redeem Israel
From all his iniquities.

PSALM 131

Childlike Trust in the LORD.
A Song of Ascents, of David.

1 O LORD, my heart is not
proud, nor my eyes haughty;
Nor do I involve myself in
great matters,
Or in things too difficult for
me.

2 Surely I have composed and
quieted my soul;
Like a weaned child *rests*
against his mother,

My soul is like a weaned child
within me.
3 O Israel, hope in the LORD
From this time forth and
forever.

PSALM 132

Prayer for the LORD's Blessing
upon the Sanctuary.
A Song of Ascents.

1 Remember, O LORD, on
David's behalf,
All his affliction;
2 How he swore to the LORD
And vowed to the Mighty One
of Jacob,
3 "Surely I will not enter my
house,
Nor lie on my bed;
4 I will not give sleep to my eyes
Or slumber to my eyelids,
5 Until I find a place for the
LORD,
A dwelling place for the
Mighty One of Jacob."
6 Behold, we heard of it in
Ephrathah,
We found it in the field of
Jaar.
7 Let us go into His dwelling
place;
Let us worship at His
footstool.
8 Arise, O LORD, to Your resting
place,
You and the ark of Your
strength.
9 Let Your priests be clothed
with righteousness,
And let Your godly ones sing
for joy.
10 For the sake of David Your
servant,
Do not turn away the face of
Your anointed.
11 The LORD has sworn to David

A truth from which He will
not turn back:
"Of the fruit of your body I will
set upon your throne.
12 "If your sons will keep My
covenant
And My testimony which I
will teach them,
Their sons also shall sit upon
your throne forever."
13 For the LORD has chosen Zion;
He has desired it for His
habitation.
14 "This is My resting place
forever;
Here I will dwell, for I have
desired it.
15 "I will abundantly bless her
provision;
I will satisfy her needy with
bread.
16 "Her priests also I will clothe
with salvation,
And her godly ones will sing
aloud for joy.
17 "There I will cause the horn of
David to spring forth;
I have prepared a lamp for
Mine anointed.
18 "His enemies I will clothe with
shame,
But upon himself his crown
shall shine."

PSALM 133

The Excellency of
Brotherly Unity.
A Song of Ascents, of David.

1 Behold, how good and how
pleasant it is
For brothers to dwell together
in unity!
2 It is like the precious oil upon
the head,
Coming down upon the beard,
Even Aaron's beard,

Coming down upon the edge
of his robes.
3 It is like the dew of Hermon
Coming down upon the
mountains of Zion;
For there the LORD
commanded the
blessing—life forever.

PSALM 134

Greetings of Night Watchers.
A Song of Ascents.

1 Behold, bless the LORD, all
servants of the LORD,
Who serve by night in the
house of the LORD!
2 Lift up your hands to the
sanctuary
And bless the LORD.
3 May the LORD bless you from
Zion,
He who made heaven and
earth.

PSALM 135

Praise the LORD's Wonderful
Works. Vanity of Idols.

1 Praise the LORD!
Praise the name of the LORD;
Praise *Him*, O servants of the
LORD,
2 You who stand in the house of
the LORD,
In the courts of the house of
our God!
3 Praise the LORD, for the LORD
is good;
Sing praises to His name, for it
is lovely.
4 For the LORD has chosen
Jacob for Himself,
Israel for His own possession.
5 For I know that the LORD is
great
And that our Lord is above all
gods.

6 Whatever the LORD pleases,
He does,
In heaven and in earth, in the
seas and in all deeps.
7 He causes the vapors to
ascend from the ends of the
earth;
Who makes lightnings for the
rain,
Who brings forth the wind
from His treasuries.
8 He smote the firstborn of
Egypt,
Both of man and beast.
9 He sent signs and wonders
into your midst, O Egypt,
Upon Pharaoh and all his
servants.
10 He smote many nations
And slew mighty kings,
11 Sihon, king of the Amorites,
And Og, king of Bashan,
And all the kingdoms of
Canaan;
12 And He gave their land as a
heritage,
A heritage to Israel His
people.
13 Your name, O LORD, is
everlasting,
Your remembrance, O LORD,
throughout all generations.
14 For the LORD will judge His
people
And will have compassion on
His servants.
15 The idols of the nations are
but silver and gold,
The work of man's hands.
16 They have mouths, but they
do not speak;
They have eyes, but they do
not see;
17 They have ears, but they do
not hear,
Nor is there any breath at all
in their mouths.

18 Those who make them will be like them,
Yes, everyone who trusts in them.

19 O house of Israel, bless the LORD;
O house of Aaron, bless the LORD;

20 O house of Levi, bless the LORD;
You who [1]revere the LORD, bless the LORD.

21 Blessed be the LORD from Zion,
Who dwells in Jerusalem.
Praise the LORD!

PSALM 136

Thanks for the LORD's Goodness to Israel.

1 Give thanks to the LORD, for He is good,
For His lovingkindness is everlasting.

2 Give thanks to the God of gods,
For His lovingkindness is everlasting.

3 Give thanks to the Lord of lords,
For His lovingkindness is everlasting.

4 To Him who alone does great wonders,
For His lovingkindness is everlasting;

5 To Him who made the heavens with skill,
For His lovingkindness is everlasting;

6 To Him who spread out the earth above the waters,
For His lovingkindness is everlasting;

7 To Him who made *the* great lights,
For His lovingkindness is everlasting:

8 The sun to rule by day,
For His lovingkindness is everlasting,

9 The moon and stars to rule by night,
For His lovingkindness is everlasting.

10 To Him who smote the Egyptians in their firstborn,
For His lovingkindness is everlasting,

11 And brought Israel out from their midst,
For His lovingkindness is everlasting,

12 With a strong hand and an outstretched arm,
For His lovingkindness is everlasting.

13 To Him who divided the Red Sea asunder,
For His lovingkindness is everlasting,

14 And made Israel pass through the midst of it,
For His lovingkindness is everlasting;

15 But He overthrew Pharaoh and his army in the Red Sea,
For His lovingkindness is everlasting.

16 To Him who led His people through the wilderness,
For His lovingkindness is everlasting;

17 To Him who smote great kings,
For His lovingkindness is everlasting,

18 And slew mighty kings,
For His lovingkindness is everlasting:

---

1. Lit *fear*

19 Sihon, king of the Amorites,
For His lovingkindness is
everlasting,

20 And Og, king of Bashan,
For His lovingkindness is
everlasting,

21 And gave their land as a
heritage,
For His lovingkindness is
everlasting,

22 Even a heritage to Israel His
servant,
For His lovingkindness is
everlasting.

23 Who remembered us in our
low estate,
For His lovingkindness is
everlasting,

24 And has rescued us from our
adversaries,
For His lovingkindness is
everlasting;

25 Who gives food to all flesh,
For His lovingkindness is
everlasting.

26 Give thanks to the God of
heaven,
For His lovingkindness is
everlasting.

PSALM 137

An Experience of the Captivity.

1 By the rivers of Babylon,
There we sat down and wept,
When we remembered Zion.

2 Upon the willows in the midst
of it
We hung our harps.

3 For there our captors
demanded of us songs,
And our tormentors mirth,
saying,
"Sing us one of the songs of
Zion."

4 How can we sing the LORD's
song

In a foreign land?

5 If I forget you, O Jerusalem,
May my right hand forget *her
skill.*

6 May my tongue cling to the
roof of my mouth
If I do not remember you,
If I do not exalt Jerusalem
Above my chief joy.

7 Remember, O LORD, against
the sons of Edom
The day of Jerusalem,
Who said, "Raze it, raze it
To its very foundation."

8 O daughter of Babylon, you
devastated one,
How blessed will be the one
who repays you
With the recompense with
which you have repaid us.

9 How blessed will be the one
who seizes and dashes your
little ones
Against the rock.

PSALM 138

*Thanksgiving for the
LORD's Favor.
A Psalm of David.*

1 I will give You thanks with all
my heart;
I will sing praises to You
before the gods.

2 I will bow down toward Your
holy temple
And give thanks to Your name
for Your lovingkindness and
Your truth;
For You have magnified Your
word according to all Your
name.

3 On the day I called, You
answered me;
You made me bold with
strength in my soul.

117

4 All the kings of the earth will
give thanks to You, O Lord,
When they have heard the
words of Your mouth.

5 And they will sing of the ways
of the Lord,
For great is the glory of the
Lord.

6 For though the Lord is
exalted,
Yet He regards the lowly,
But the haughty He knows
from afar.

7 Though I walk in the midst of
trouble, You will revive me;
You will stretch forth Your
hand against the wrath of my
enemies,
And Your right hand will save
me.

8 The Lord will accomplish
what concerns me;
Your lovingkindness, O Lord,
is everlasting;
Do not forsake the works of
Your hands.

PSALM 139

*God's Omnipresence
and Omniscience.*
For the choir director.
A Psalm of David.

1 O Lord, You have searched
me and known *me.*

2 You know when I sit down
and when I rise up;
You understand my thought
from afar.

3 You scrutinize my path and
my lying down,
And are intimately acquainted
with all my ways.

4 Even before there is a word on
my tongue,

Behold, O Lord, You know it
all.

5 You have enclosed me behind
and before,
And laid Your hand upon me.

6 *Such* knowledge is too
wonderful for me;
It is *too* high, I cannot attain
to it.

7 Where can I go from Your
Spirit?
Or where can I flee from Your
presence?

8 If I ascend to heaven, You are
there;
If I make my bed in Sheol,
behold, You are there.

9 If I take the wings of the
dawn,
If I dwell in the remotest part
of the sea,

10 Even there Your hand will
lead me,
And Your right hand will lay
hold of me.

11 If I say, "Surely the darkness
will overwhelm me,
And the light around me will
be night,"

12 Even the darkness is not dark
to You,
And the night is as bright as
the day.
Darkness and light are alike *to
You.*

13 For You formed my inward
parts;
You wove me in my mother's
womb.

14 I will give thanks to You, for [1]I
am fearfully and wonderfully
made;
Wonderful are Your works,
And my soul knows it very
well.

1. Some ancient versions read *You are fearfully wonderful*

15 My frame was not hidden
from You,
When I was made in secret,
And skillfully wrought in the
depths of the earth;
16 Your eyes have seen my
unformed substance;
And in Your book were all
written
The days that were ordained
for me,
When as yet there was not one
of them.
17 How precious also are Your
thoughts to me, O God!
How vast is the sum of them!
18 If I should count them, they
would outnumber the sand.
When I awake, I am still with
You.
19 O that You would slay the
wicked, O God;
Depart from me, therefore,
men of bloodshed.
20 For they speak against You
wickedly,
And Your enemies take *Your
name* in vain.
21 Do I not hate those who hate
You, O Lord?
And do I not loathe those who
rise up against You?
22 I hate them with the utmost
hatred;
They have become my
enemies.
23 Search me, O God, and know
my heart;
Try me and know my anxious
thoughts;
24 And see if there be any hurtful
way in me,
And lead me in the everlasting
way.

---

1. Lit *push violently*

PSALM 140

*Prayer for Protection
against the Wicked.*
For the choir director.
A Psalm of David.

1 Rescue me, O Lord, from evil
men;
Preserve me from violent men
2 Who devise evil things in *their*
hearts;
They continually stir up wars.
3 They sharpen their tongues as
a serpent;
Poison of a viper is under their
lips.   Selah.
4 Keep me, O Lord, from the
hands of the wicked;
Preserve me from violent men
Who have purposed to ¹trip
up my feet.
5 The proud have hidden a trap
for me, and cords;
They have spread a net by the
wayside;
They have set snares for me.
Selah.
6 I said to the Lord, "You are
my God;
Give ear, O Lord, to the voice
of my supplications.
7"O God the Lord, the strength
of my salvation,
You have covered my head in
the day of battle.
8"Do not grant, O Lord, the
desires of the wicked;
Do not promote his *evil*
device, *that* they *not* be
exalted.   Selah.
9"As for the head of those who
surround me,
May the mischief of their lips
cover them.
10"May burning coals fall upon
them;

119

May they be cast into the fire,
Into deep pits from which they
cannot rise.

11 "May a slanderer not be
established in the earth;
May evil hunt the violent man
[1]speedily."

12 I know that the LORD will
maintain the cause of the
afflicted
And justice for the poor.

13 Surely the righteous will give
thanks to Your name;
The upright will dwell in Your
presence.

PSALM 141

*An Evening Prayer for
Sanctification and Protection.*
A Psalm of David.

1 O LORD, I call upon You;
hasten to me!
Give ear to my voice when I
call to You!

2 May my prayer be counted as
incense before You;
The lifting up of my hands as
the evening offering.

3 Set a guard, O LORD, over my
mouth;
Keep watch over the door of
my lips.

4 Do not incline my heart to any
evil thing,
To practice deeds of
wickedness
With men who do iniquity;
And do not let me eat of their
delicacies.

5 Let the righteous smite me in
kindness and reprove me;
It is oil upon the head;
Do not let my head refuse it,
For still my prayer is against
their wicked deeds.

6 Their judges are thrown down
by the sides of the rock,
And they hear my words, for
they are pleasant.

7 As when one plows and breaks
open the earth,
Our bones have been scattered
at the mouth of Sheol.

8 For my eyes are toward You,
O GOD, the Lord;
In You I take refuge; do not
leave me defenseless.

9 Keep me from the jaws of the
trap which they have set for
me,
And from the snares of those
who do iniquity.

10 Let the wicked fall into their
own nets,
While I pass by safely.

PSALM 142

Prayer for Help in Trouble.
Maskil of David, when he was in
the cave. A Prayer.

1 I cry aloud with my voice to
the LORD;
I make supplication with my
voice to the LORD.

2 I pour out my complaint
before Him;
I declare my trouble before
Him.

3 When my spirit was
overwhelmed within me,
You knew my path.
In the way where I walk
They have hidden a trap for
me.

4 Look to the right and see;
For there is no one who
regards me;
There is no escape for me;
No one cares for my soul.

5 I cried out to You, O LORD;

---

1. Lit *thrust upon thrust*

I said, "You are my refuge,
My portion in the land of the
living.
6 "Give heed to my cry,
For I am brought very low;
Deliver me from my
persecutors,
For they are too strong for me.
7 "Bring my soul out of prison,
So that I may give thanks to
Your name;
The righteous will surround
me,
For You will deal bountifully
with me."

PSALM 143

*Prayer for Deliverance
and Guidance.*
A Psalm of David.

1 Hear my prayer, O LORD,
Give ear to my supplications!
Answer me in Your
faithfulness, in Your
righteousness!
2 And do not enter into
judgment with Your servant,
For in Your sight no man
living is righteous.
3 For the enemy has persecuted
my soul;
He has crushed my life to the
ground;
He has made me dwell in dark
places, like those who have
long been dead.
4 Therefore my spirit is
overwhelmed within me;
My heart is ¹appalled within
me.
5 I remember the days of old;
I meditate on all Your doings;
I muse on the work of Your
hands.
6 I stretch out my hands to You;

My soul *longs* for You, as a
parched land.   Selah.
7 Answer me quickly, O LORD,
my spirit fails;
Do not hide Your face from
me,
Or I will become like those
who go down to the pit.
8 Let me hear Your
lovingkindness in the
morning;
For I trust in You;
Teach me the way in which I
should walk;
For to You I lift up my soul.
9 Deliver me, O LORD, from my
enemies;
I take refuge in You.
10 Teach me to do Your will,
For You are my God;
Let Your good Spirit lead me
on level ground.
11 For the sake of Your name, O
LORD, revive me.
In Your righteousness bring
my soul out of trouble.
12 And in Your lovingkindness,
cut off my enemies
And destroy all those who
afflict my soul,
For I am Your servant.

PSALM 144

Prayer for Rescue and Prosperity.
A Psalm of David.

1 Blessed be the LORD, my rock,
Who trains my hands for war,
And my fingers for battle;
2 My lovingkindness and my
fortress,
My stronghold and my
deliverer,
My shield and He in whom I
take refuge,

1. Or *desolate*

121

Who subdues my people
under me.

3 O Lord, what is man, that
You take knowledge of him?
Or the son of man, that You
think of him?

4 Man is like a mere breath;
His days are like a passing
shadow.

5 Bow Your heavens, O Lord,
and come down;
Touch the mountains, that
they may smoke.

6 Flash forth lightning and
scatter them;
Send out Your arrows and
confuse them.

7 Stretch forth Your hand from
on high;
Rescue me and deliver me out
of great waters,
Out of the hand of aliens

8 Whose mouths speak deceit,
And whose right hand is a
right hand of falsehood.

9 I will sing a new song to You,
O God;
Upon a harp of ten strings I
will sing praises to You,

10 Who gives salvation to kings,
Who rescues David His
servant from the evil sword.

11 Rescue me and deliver me out
of the hand of aliens,
Whose mouth speaks deceit
And whose right hand is a
right hand of falsehood.

12 Let our sons in their youth be
as grown-up plants,
And our daughters as corner
pillars fashioned as for a
palace;

13 Let our garners be full,
furnishing every kind of
produce,
And our flocks bring forth

thousands and ten thousands
in our fields;

14 Let our cattle bear
Without mishap and without
loss,
Let there be no outcry in our
streets!

15 How blessed are the people
who are so situated;
How blessed are the people
whose God is the Lord!

PSALM 145

*The Lord Extolled for
His Goodness.*
A Psalm of Praise, of David.

1 I will extol You, my God, O
King,
And I will bless Your name
forever and ever.

2 Every day I will bless You,
And I will praise Your name
forever and ever.

3 Great is the Lord, and highly
to be praised,
And His greatness is
unsearchable.

4 One generation shall praise
Your works to another,
And shall declare Your
mighty acts.

5 On the glorious splendor of
Your majesty
And on Your wonderful
works, I will meditate.

6 Men shall speak of the power
of Your awesome acts,
And I will tell of Your
greatness.

7 They shall eagerly utter the
memory of Your abundant
goodness
And will shout joyfully of
Your righteousness.

8 The Lord is gracious and
merciful;

Slow to anger and great in
lovingkindness.

9 The LORD is good to all,
And His mercies are over all
His works.

10 All Your works shall give
thanks to You, O LORD,
And Your godly ones shall
bless You.

11 They shall speak of the glory
of Your kingdom
And talk of Your power;

12 To make known to the sons of
men Your mighty acts
And the glory of the majesty
of Your kingdom.

13 Your kingdom is an
everlasting kingdom,
And Your dominion *endures*
throughout all generations.

14 The LORD sustains all who fall
And raises up all who are
bowed down.

15 The eyes of all look to You,
And You give them their food
in due time.

16 You open Your hand
And satisfy the desire of every
living thing.

17 The LORD is righteous in all
His ways
And kind in all His deeds.

18 The LORD is near to all who
call upon Him,
To all who call upon Him in
truth.

19 He will fulfill the desire of
those who fear Him;
He will also hear their cry and
will save them.

20 The LORD keeps all who love
Him,
But all the wicked He will
destroy.

21 My mouth will speak the
praise of the LORD,

And all flesh will bless His
holy name forever and ever.

PSALM 146

The LORD an Abundant Helper.

1 Praise the LORD!
Praise the LORD, O my soul!

2 I will praise the LORD while I
live;
I will sing praises to my God
while I have my being.

3 Do not trust in princes,
In mortal man, in whom there
is no salvation.

4 His spirit departs, he returns
to the earth;
In that very day his thoughts
perish.

5 How blessed is he whose help
is the God of Jacob,
Whose hope is in the LORD his
God,

6 Who made heaven and earth,
The sea and all that is in them;
Who keeps faith forever;

7 Who executes justice for the
oppressed;
Who gives food to the hungry.
The LORD sets the prisoners
free.

8 The LORD opens *the eyes of* the
blind;
The LORD raises up those who
are bowed down;
The LORD loves the righteous;

9 The LORD protects the
strangers;
He supports the fatherless and
the widow,
But He thwarts the way of the
wicked.

10 The LORD will reign forever,
Your God, O Zion, to all
generations.
Praise the LORD!

PSALM 147

Praise for Jerusalem's
Restoration and Prosperity.

1 Praise the LORD!
For it is good to sing praises to
our God;
For [1]it is pleasant *and* praise is
becoming.

2 The LORD builds up
Jerusalem;
He gathers the outcasts of
Israel.

3 He heals the brokenhearted
And binds up their [2]wounds.

4 He counts the number of the
stars;
He gives names to all of them.

5 Great is our Lord and
abundant in strength;
His understanding is infinite.

6 The LORD [3]supports the
afflicted;
He brings down the wicked to
the ground.

7 Sing to the LORD with
thanksgiving;
Sing praises to our God on the
lyre,

8 Who covers the heavens with
clouds,
Who provides rain for the
earth,
Who makes grass to grow on
the mountains.

9 He gives to the beast its food,
And to the young ravens
which cry.

10 He does not delight in the
strength of the horse;
He does not take pleasure in
the legs of a man.

11 The LORD favors those who
fear Him,
Those who wait for His
lovingkindness.

12 Praise the LORD, O Jerusalem!
Praise your God, O Zion!

13 For He has strengthened the
bars of your gates;
He has blessed your sons
within you.

14 He makes peace in your
borders;
He satisfies you with the finest
of the wheat.

15 He sends forth His command
to the earth;
His word runs very swiftly.

16 He gives snow like wool;
He scatters the frost like ashes.

17 He casts forth His ice as
fragments;
Who can stand before His
cold?

18 He sends forth His word and
melts them;
He causes His wind to blow
and the waters to flow.

19 He declares His words to
Jacob,
His statutes and His
ordinances to Israel.

20 He has not dealt thus with any
nation;
And as for His ordinances,
they have not known them.
Praise the LORD!

PSALM 148

The Whole Creation Invoked
to Praise the LORD.

1 Praise the LORD!
Praise the LORD from the
heavens;
Praise Him in the heights!

2 Praise Him, all His angels;
Praise Him, all His hosts!

3 Praise Him, sun and moon;
Praise Him, all stars of light!

4 Praise Him, highest heavens,

1. Or *He is gracious* 2. Lit *sorrows* 3. Or *relieves*

124

And the waters that are above
the heavens!
5 Let them praise the name of
the LORD,
For He commanded and they
were created.
6 He has also established them
forever and ever;
He has made a decree which
will not pass away.
7 Praise the LORD from the
earth,
Sea monsters and all deeps;
8 Fire and hail, snow and
clouds;
Stormy wind, fulfilling His
word;
9 Mountains and all hills;
Fruit trees and all cedars;
10 Beasts and all cattle;
Creeping things and winged
fowl;
11 Kings of the earth and all
peoples;
Princes and all judges of the
earth;
12 Both young men and virgins;
Old men and children.
13 Let them praise the name of
the LORD,
For His name alone is exalted;
His glory is above earth and
heaven.
14 And He has lifted up a horn
for His people,
Praise for all His godly ones;
Even for the sons of Israel, a
people near to Him.
Praise the LORD!

PSALM 149

*Israel Invoked to
Praise the LORD.*

1 Praise the LORD!
Sing to the LORD a new song,
And His praise in the
congregation of the godly
ones.
2 Let Israel be glad in his
Maker;
Let the sons of Zion rejoice in
their King.
3 Let them praise His name with
dancing;
Let them sing praises to Him
with timbrel and lyre.
4 For the LORD takes pleasure in
His people;
He will beautify the afflicted
ones with salvation.
5 Let the godly ones exult in
glory;
Let them sing for joy on their
beds.
6 *Let* the high praises of God *be*
in their mouth,
And a two-edged sword in
their hand,
7 To execute vengeance on the
nations
And punishment on the
peoples,
8 To bind their kings with
chains
And their nobles with fetters
of iron,
9 To execute on them the
judgment written;
This is an honor for all His
godly ones.
Praise the LORD!

PSALM 150

A Psalm of Praise.

1 Praise the LORD!
Praise God in His sanctuary;
Praise Him in His mighty
expanse.
2 Praise Him for His mighty
deeds;

125

Praise Him according to His
excellent greatness.
3 Praise Him with trumpet
sound;
Praise Him with harp and
lyre.
4 Praise Him with timbrel and
dancing;

Praise Him with stringed
instruments and pipe.
5 Praise Him with loud cymbals;
Praise Him with resounding
cymbals.
6 Let everything that has breath
praise the LORD.
Praise the LORD!